LEGACY

OF

TREES

LEGACY
OF
TREES

Purposeful Wandering in Vancouver's Stanley Park

Nina Shoroplova

Heritage House Publishing Company Ltd.
heritagehouse.ca

Cataloguing information available from Library and Archives Canada

978-1-77203-303-8 (PBK)
978-1-77203-304-5 (EBOOK)

Edited by Marial Shea
Proofread by Grace Yaginuma
Index by Martin Gavin
Cover, interior book design, and maps by Jacqui Thomas
Cover photographs: Andrew Dunlop / iStockphoto.com (*front*),
zennie / iStockphoto.com (*back*)
Frontispiece photograph: Milan Rademakers / shutterstock.com
Interior colour photographs by Nina Shoroplova
Interior historical photographs are from the City of Vancouver
Archives unless otherwise noted

The interior of this book was produced on FSC®-certified, acid-free paper,
processed chlorine-free, and printed with vegetable-based inks.

Heritage House gratefully acknowledges that the land on which we live and work is within
the traditional territories of the Lkwungen (Esquimalt and Songhees), Malahat, Pacheedaht,
Scia'new, T'Sou-ke, and W̱SÁNEĆ (Pauquachin, Tsartlip, Tsawout, and Tseycum) Peoples.

We also acknowledge that Stanley Park, the subject of this book, is located on the
unceded territories of the Musqueam, Squamish, and Tsleil-Waututh Peoples.

We acknowledge the financial support of the Government of Canada through the Canada
Book Fund (CBF) and the Canada Council for the Arts, and the Province of British
Columbia through the British Columbia Arts Council and the Book Publishing Tax Credit.

24 23 22 21 20 1 2 3 4 5

Printed in China

To all who visit Stanley Park, tread softly.
And may you enjoy and love this park as much as I do.

Contents

PART III

List of Maps

Foreword

IN ALL MY years working for the Vancouver Park Board, my favourite days have been those spent in Stanley Park. It is a place in which to move around, with rewards and surprises around every corner at each passing season. I will never grow tired of the powerful life force that emanates from its coastal rainforest heart. It spreads in finger-like extensions through ornamental and exotic plant collections, sports fields, and beaches, until eventually it hits the concrete wall that is Vancouver's West End. Travelling in the opposite direction, we leave the world of responsibilities and artificial constructs to melt into its natural sights, sounds, and smells, to stabilize our brain chemicals, and to bathe in serenity and beauty until our inner nature can be touched.

When Nina Shoroplova came to me with her new manuscript *Legacy of Trees*, I had the rare treat of starting a read by an author previously unknown to me; she was writing about a place that has been a central theme in my life. Books about Vancouver and books about trees fill my shelves, but not one evokes memories as this one does—memories of wandering through Stanley Park.

What *Legacy of Trees* accomplishes is a wedding of passage through time and passage through space. It pulls into time and space the works of people like Vancouver's early archivist Major James Matthews, who spent his lifetime chronicling events during the city's formative years. His work in the early twentieth century explored its long story through conversations with August Jack Khahtsahlano, and continued through its occasionally dark colonial establishment period. Many of the trees Major Matthews wrote about are still here in some form or another.

Legacy of Trees teaches us how to watch for the subtle hints of traditional usage while we walk in the forest. With that information, it is possible to walk with eyes open to the centuries of pre-colonization and traditional land use. We learn about the townsites that were present on this peninsula since time immemorial. And there are more recent stories to learn. Until reading this book, I never knew the disturbing tale behind the grove of trees where I conduct my annual springtime cherry blossom tour, the very trees the Uyeda family donated to the Park Board shortly before being sent to a Japanese internment camp during the Second World War.

This book is also scientifically literate. Whether exploring the timber uses of the forest in the early days, the natural history of rhododendrons, or the mystery of the fungal mycelial mats connecting trees into neural networks, one cannot help but learn new things as one turns the pages.

Here's how I suggest you use this book. Read it first in a leisurely manner at home, and internalize the park's history since its dedication in 1888. Then tuck it into your backpack and take it with you as a companion on your park wanderings. Take it on your smartphone or tablet as an ebook. Follow its maps, and use a maps app to enter the latitude/longitude coordinates of your place of interest for the day. Re-read its tales in the presence of the very trees about which it speaks, time travel with them, and return to the city with a richer sense of the connections between the trees of this great park and its human and animal actors. Then repeat... This book will entertain you through many wanderings.

I highly recommend *Legacy of Trees* to anyone who loves Stanley Park, and to anyone who loves trees. It is written with scientific integrity and historical accuracy, but also with a flow that allows for easy and enjoyable reading. It can become your companion on many happy sojourns in the world's greatest urban park. Through *Legacy of Trees*, we have a snapshot of Stanley Park's first 130-plus years as told through its trees. Perhaps most importantly, we have an informative historical chapter to remember as we turn the corner and enter a process of reconciliation between the region's Indigenous Peoples and the Vancouver Park Board, a process aimed at creating a deeper and better vision of how the park will move forward into the future.

Bill Stephen,
SUPERINTENDENT OF URBAN FORESTRY (RETIRED),
VANCOUVER BOARD OF PARKS AND RECREATION

Introduction

Purposeful Wandering

IN THE GORGEOUSLY colourful fall of 2017, I had a sudden thought: "I live next to Stanley Park, one of the world's most beloved and best parks. How have I not noticed?" Of course I had *noticed*, but I hadn't taken that awareness deep inside. I barely *knew* the park. I have lived beside this park for twenty-five years. I first saw the crescent beach of English Bay and the storytelling totems in the park in 1961, fifty-nine years ago. Have I been asleep? Can I wake up? Is it time?

If I am going to get to know this park—this Stanley Park—and call it "my park," I will have to wander it purposefully, path by path, plaque by plaque, monument by monument, rock by rock, tree by tree, trail by trail, blossom by flowering blossom, through every season, and allow its layers of history to seep into me as though it were a living, breathing being.

Actually, it is.

The Trees in My Life

Whatever place I have called home during each stage of my life, that place and time has been associated with a specific tree or trees. I only came to realize that recently. Maybe it's the same for you. What are the trees you can see from your window? In your backyard? Which is your favourite tree in your nearest park?

Growing up in Wales, I was a Brownie (seven- and eight-year-old girls on the path to becoming Girl Guides). My Brownie leader—the Brown Owl—taught me about the common English oak trees growing in Roath Park beside our local library in Penylan, Cardiff. I learned to recognize the oak trees' acorns and their five- to seven-lobed leaves.

When I entered high school in Llandaff, aged eleven, I chatted with my girlfriends in the playground under the shelter of several massive horse chestnut trees. Their shiny brown conkers were appealing to the touch and decidedly collectible.

When I first married and lived at Douglas Lake Ranch in the province of British Columbia—having by then immigrated to Canada—my home was surrounded by tall black cottonwoods. This member of the poplar family has a habit of constantly dropping bits of itself: yellow-green pollen that aggravated family allergies, red blooms that stained the front path, cotton-covered seeds that made it look as though it had snowed, little branches, big branches, and finally leaves, millions and millions of leaves. These cottonwoods also spread out their roots to ensure they gained all possible goodness from the soil; it was difficult to grow anything much in that garden.

Living in Australia during the first half of the 1980s, I fell in love with the "gum trees"— the eucalyptus trees—with all of them. These flowering evergreens express their individuality through their twisted, irregular shapes, peeling barks, variety of colourful blossoms, and aromatic resin. They absolutely called to my soul. I also loved the many weeping willows that hugged the banks of a tiny stream below our house on our sheep and cattle property.

When I returned to Canada, my parents immigrated to BC too, to Victoria, BC's capital city on Vancouver Island. Victoria is one of the few places in Canada where the arbutus tree grows really well. Although eucalyptus trees and arbutus trees belong to two different families (Myrtaceae and Ericaceae), they have many common features, at least in this high school botanist's eye, such as an irregularly shaped trunk and peeling bark. So, naturally, I also fell in love with the arbutus trees during the three years Victoria was my home.

In the grounds of my home in Vernon, in the Okanagan Valley, grew a mature *Ginkgo biloba* tree, a unique holdover genus from 270 million years ago—that is, *before* the days of the dinosaurs. Unmistakable fan-shaped leaves grow closely around each branch, tracing its shape; some call them butterfly leaves. One fall, every yellowed leaf on our ginkgo fell to the ground overnight, and the next day we took our family Christmas card photograph standing on a yellow carpet provided by nature.

For a while, the place I called home was shifting, and I don't remember any particular trees. Perhaps it is the trees that tell me I am home and it's time to spread my roots down and my branches out and up.

Now living in Vancouver's West End many decades later, I identify with a full range of trees. The myriad of maples planted along the city's sidewalks are glorious in their fall colours, with leaves ranging from the size of a loonie (one of the Japanese cultivars) to that of a large dinner plate (the native bigleaf maples). The magnificent Caucasian wingnut on the corner of Comox and Chilco Streets is well over a hundred years old. The giant red oak in Alexandra Park, overlooking English Bay from the corner of Beach Avenue and Bidwell Street, is a West End icon. Witch hazel trees, with their constantly changing summer and fall palette, their early spring brightness, and their intoxicating scent, are among my favourites. Black locust trees, with their brilliant yellow fall colour and their big seed pods, are proud against the sky. And the enormous weeping willows at Second Beach invite one to relax.

One tree demands special attention, the weeping beech at the top end of the Shakespeare Garden in Stanley Park. When I first walked under its canopy of falling dark green drapery, tears came to my eyes. Somehow, the generosity of that tree, offering its shade and comfort to all who stand, walk, and drive underneath its south-facing leaves, opened my heart.

As a friend says, "Trees are divine beings."

That weeping beech reminded me of the moment in James Cameron's movie *Avatar* when the Na'vi princess Neytiri takes Jake Sully to *utraya mokri*—the Tree of Voices—so that he too might hear the prayers of the ancestors. Before James Cameron wrote what became the climactic love scene in *Avatar*, he must have visited Stanley Park's most special weeping beech, with its hanging green boughs.

I Set Myself a Challenge

I decided to write this book about the legacy trees of Stanley Park so I could wander purposefully, familiarize myself with the park, and learn that there is more to the park than the totem poles, lighthouses, seawall, shoreline, and views of Vancouver. I intended to learn about the world-famous temperate coastal rainforest that is teeming with western hemlocks, western redcedars, western yews (also called Pacific yews), Douglas-firs, Sitka spruce, vine maples, bigleaf maples, red alders, paper birches, black cottonwoods, cascaras, wild bitter cherry trees, and Pacific crabapple trees. I proposed to acquaint myself with the shrubs and herbs that create the varied understorey.

I have read that this old-growth forest provides a natural habitat for raccoons, skunks, moles, voles, beavers, bats, and squirrels (black and grey squirrels, northern

This almost-logged Douglas-fir hosts a bald eagle's aerie.

flying squirrels, and Douglas squirrels). Its woody debris (snags, nurse logs, and root wads) provides a home for birds and insects, mould and lichen. Its soil is teeming with life too small to see, as is the soil of every forest.

So, since September 6, 2017, I have been walking in the park two or three days a week, for an hour or two and more, getting to know the park and its trees. I realized I could hardly tell them apart. "What is that tree? Is that a ...?" I wanted to learn the names of the trees.

As I walked, I wondered how things used to be, how they could have grown into what I see now, how the park has changed into its present presence, and sometimes I walked to find something that will be there or might be there, or was once there and is no longer. When I arrived back home, I would research the plants I'd photographed, the plaques I'd uncovered, the history I'd surmised, and the people who are here no longer.

The overarching constant that influences the life of Stanley Park is that this park and its trees are constantly changing, adapting, restoring, recovering, and evolving. The history of this peninsula, including the time before it was a park, has been layered by interference from weather, flora, and fauna, especially humans. Gradually, I realized that the trees now growing in Stanley Park reflect the beliefs and values of the Vancouver Board of Parks and Recreation since Stanley Park was first named in 1888. The history of the trees is also the history of the park as a whole. And the citizens of Vancouver influence those beliefs and values. As Vancouver changes, so does the park.

What is the park telling us Vancouverites about ourselves?

Let us stroll or cycle or drive from tree to tree in this world-famous park, which passed its 130th birthday on September 27, 2018. Let's discover its very special trees—special because they were planted to commemorate a specific event, or for no particular reason, or because they have been here all along, growing where their germinated seeds fell to the forest floor.

What can I say? I'm here for the trees.

How This Book Is Organized

I am more likely to tell you about the planting of a tree than about its original homeland, about its park history rather than its height, its influence rather than the measurement of its girth. I include a tree's Latin name where I could figure it out by using apps and asking those more knowledgeable than me; its latitude and longitude (with Google Maps, "latitude 49.2997 N | longitude 123.1339 W" can be entered as "49.2997, -123.1339"); and its best feature (as far as I'm concerned). If the tree is on a trail, I give you the name of the trail.

The trees described in *Legacy of Trees* are included because they:

- are remembered through historic interviews or photographs;
- were planted to commemorate an event, a person, or a date, and may or may not have a plaque to prove it;
- were planted to add beauty and intrigue;
- hold or held a record;
- are special;
- represent one stage of a tree's life;
- represent a species.

I've separated the tree stories into three parts comprising a total of thirty-three chapters. The parts are arranged chronologically and geographically. Chapters 1 to 12 in Part I describe trees that were already growing on the peninsula headland that became the federal reserve and then became Stanley Park.

The chapters within Parts II and III are arranged chronologically according to tree planting dates. Chapters 13 to 27 in Part II describe the most strongly colonial and imperial years of the park, up until 1960. I became a teenager in the sixties and it seems the park did too, becoming more independent from its British parent and taking more of a responsible role within Canada. Chapters 28 to 33 of Part III cover the years of growing independence.

Most chapters relate to a specific date and place, but some provide general park information. Some describe trees that can only be read about or seen in old photographs from Vancouver's archives, yet I've

Stanley Park in 1911. Each number corresponds to a chapter of this book.

still included those chapter numbers in the facing map.[1] Chapter 6, "Fire!," takes place away from Stanley Park, but its events influence the park's story. Other chapters describe events taking place throughout the park whose effects are visible in multiple locations, especially on many of the trails; for example, the number 10 (for chapter 10, "Trail Trees") appears in several places on the map.

I used this map because I was intrigued by the contrast between the 1911 uses of the park (see the labels "Deer and Goats," "Landing Pier," "Summer House," and "Bath House") and today's uses. If you would prefer to look at up-to-date maps of the park, the City of Vancouver makes several available online.[2]

The list below tells you which parts of the park can be seen in one visit (with the corresponding chapters in order of the route), as you walk or cycle or rollerblade through the park. There are plenty of benches, picnic tables, public washrooms, cafés, and restaurants, so you can rest and refresh along the way—though not so much along the trails.

ROUTE A goes east via the **Georgia Street entrance** and the **Promenade** to the **Stanley Park Pavilion** (chapters 7, 5, 24, 28, 16) and takes one to two hours. Stop and have a drink or a meal at Stanley's Bar and Grill.

ROUTE B goes east via the Georgia Street entrance and the Promenade to the **Salmon Stream Valley** (chapters 7, 5, 24, 28, 25) and takes one to two hours. Visit the Vancouver Aquarium since you're so close.

ROUTE C goes east via the Georgia Street entrance, the Promenade, and the Salmon Stream Valley past the **Japanese-Canadian war memorial** to **Lumberman's Arch** (chapters 7, 5, 24, 28, 21). Give yourself more than two hours if it's summer and the children want to enjoy the Fox's Den Splash Park.

ROUTE D goes east via the Georgia Street entrance and the Promenade to the **Totem Pole Interpretive Centre**, **Brockton Point**, **Lumberman's Arch**, and **Chaythoos**, partly on the seawall (chapters 7, 5, 24, 19, 14, 26, 33). You have to climb above the seawall for the oak in chapter 14 and the trees in chapter 33. This route can take several hours depending on where you stop along the way. Legends of the Moon is an excellent gift shop at the Totem Pole Interpretive Centre.

ROUTE E continues counter-clockwise from Route D on **the seawall** (chapters 7, 5, 24, 19, 33, 19, 11, 19, 31, 19). This could take all day, stopping for a

A heavy snowfall in Stanley Park in November 2006.

meal at Prospect Point Bar & Grill, the Teahouse, or the concession stand at Second Beach. Alternatively, bring a picnic to share on one of the many picnic tables at, say, **Prospect Point Picnic Area** or **Ceperley Field**.

ROUTE F goes north via the Georgia Street entrance and the Promenade into the **Shakespeare and Perennial Garden** (chapters 7, 5, 24, 18, 17, 27). Allow over two hours to find all the trees. In the summer, you can also visit the Rose Garden, where something is always blooming.

ROUTE G is a seawall walk on the west side, around the **Oppenheimer bust**, past **Second Beach** and **Third Beach**, as far as **Siwash Rock** (chapters 15, 19, 31, 19, 11), and takes one to two hours.

ROUTE H is an easy walk around the Oppenheimer bust, through the **Vancouver Park Board office grounds**, and by the **putting green** in the southwest corner of the park (chapters 15, 29, 23). Give yourself several hours to identify all the trees.

ROUTE I combines the path around **Lost Lagoon** with the **Ted and Mary Greig Rhododendron Garden** (chapters 18, 30), a one- to two-hour walk at a leisurely pace.

ROUTE J can take as long as you want, combining **trails** as you please. Considering chapters 1 to 12 as you walk will evoke a strong feel for the early days of the park.

If you're visiting Stanley Park in the winter and hope to escape winter snow, you may get a shock. If you're visiting Stanley Park in the summer and think you might get too hot, realize that whereas you will cool off deep in the forest, you will also see many well-established palm trees (Chinese windmill palm, *Trachycarpus fortunei*) growing contentedly along the English Bay Beach seawall. Vancouver has the best weather in all of Canada. Of course, I may be biased.

What Stanley Park's Legacy Trees Tell Us

Learning the histories of the legacy trees in Stanley Park deepens our knowledge of the people of Vancouver—our history, our origins, our values. These stories also show how we are maturing and evolving along with the forest, the landscaped areas, and the gardens of Stanley Park. We are shaking off the colonial identity that the park exhibited for so many decades and embracing the values of reconciliation with the first inhabitants of this land, the Squamish, Musqueam, and Tsleil-Waututh. We are also reclaiming what we can of the original nature of this land while honouring our communal history.

We differ from trees in our longevity, size, life cycle, procreation methods, protection from disease, and living and dying processes. Yet I believe we can learn much from the trees around us. Trees are supportive yet ambitious, quiet yet communicative, flexible yet strong, adaptive yet true to type. Much is currently being written about flora, especially about trees' hidden ways of communicating and connecting with everything around them.

Legacy of Trees enhances our reasons for communicating and connecting with trees.

The more I talk about my love of trees with friends, the more I hear about others' love of trees. We all have our reasons to commune and be with the trees.

Share with me why you love trees at *Legacy of Trees* on my website.[3] And if you have information you think should be in this book (correcting a tree species, for instance, or informing me about a latitude and longitude or an important tree I've missed), let me know. It has been a joy to write *Legacy of Trees* and to get to know the park's trees better. I hope reading this book does the same for you.

Lace up your hiking boots or runners—we're going for a walk in Stanley Park.

PART I

The Trees Were Always There

1

The Creation of Stanley Park

Stanley Park's managers often shared a common set of assumptions regarding the park, rooted in 19th century British landscape traditions, and which generally have been respected through to the present day.

Stanley Park National Historic Site of Canada:
Commemorative Integrity Statement,
Vancouver Board of Parks and Recreation and Parks Canada, 2002

"The Most Beautiful Park in the World"

"THE TWENTY-SEVENTH OF September was a lovely day," said Major James Skitt Matthews. In a speech he gave sixty years after the official naming of Stanley Park, Vancouver's first city archivist takes us back to that lovely day in 1888 when the park was named. Let's begin our journey through the park by going back there with him:

> Cloudless sky, brilliant sunshine, cool summer zephyrs. The procession formed up at Carrall and Powell streets, where the old Maple Tree had stood. The City Band was in a wagon drawn by four horses. The Fire Brigade was in another four horse wagon. The procession proceeded via Georgia Street to the Coal Harbour bridge, and wound along the beautiful driveway twixt the trees, our Park Road. It stopped at Chaythoos, at Khahtsahlano's old home, beside Supplejack's Grave at the end of the Pipeline road where there was a grassy spot, about the only grassy spot there was. A temporary platform had been erected. Carriages, cabs, buggies, express wagons, everybody came—some on

foot. It was almost a public holiday. Many stores closed. The Hon. John Robson, of Robson Street, Provincial Secretary, the Mayor of Victoria, Mr. Abbott, of Abbott Street, C.P.R. superintendent, David Oppenheimer, the Mayor, and Park Commissioners Alexander, Ferguson, Tatlow and McCraney were there.

Two months previously, Mayor Oppenheimer had requested Sir Donald A. Smith, afterwards Lord Strathcona, to select a name. Sir Donald approached the new Governor General, Lord Stanley, who acceded to Sir Donald's suggestion. But the name had been kept a profound secret. When Mayor Oppenheimer, in a long and eloquent speech, announced [the name], the Union Jack, the national flag of Canada, was unfurled. The band played "God Save the Queen," and the assemblage gave three cheers for Her Majesty Queen Victoria. The Park Commissioners had been appointed the previous day, and Mayor Oppenheimer delivered to them a copy of the by-law creating their office, and concluded his speech by saying:

"Ladies and Gentlemen: I shall not detain you longer but, in the name of the citizens of Vancouver, I deliver Stanley Park to the care and guardianship of the Park Committee here present, and hope that under their management and that of their successors, we may ultimately realise our present hopes to have the most beautiful park in the world."

A large number of fireworks were let off which, exploding high in the air, released inflated forms of men, animals and ships to the delight of the children. Some people went picnicking, others for a drive. That night the new Salvation Army band paraded for the first time, and the day's festivities closed with a ball in the Opera House—Hart's Opera House— actually a glorified shed, on Carrall Street, in what is now our Chinatown. It was nearly daylight when the dancing ceased. It had been the most gala day Vancouver had ever known.

Major Matthews, as he was always known, had been speaking at a banquet given by the Park Board commissioners on September 27, 1948, in the Stanley Park Pavilion to commemorate Stanley Park's sixtieth anniversary.

The City's First Item of Business

The City of Vancouver was incorporated on April 6, 1886, five months after the Canadian Pacific Railway (CPR) completed its transcontinental link between Ontario and British Columbia.[1] The promise of the railway link had been part of the reason BC entered confederation with the rest of Canada in 1871.

Arthur Wellington Ross, the Liberal Member of Parliament for Lisgar, Manitoba, requested Vancouver's first city council "to petition the Dominion Government to grant Reserve on First Narrows for a City Park."[2]

That was the first item of business at the second meeting of Vancouver City Council on May 12, 1886, just thirty-six days after the city had been incorporated. You could say it was Vancouver's first-ever business item, for the first council meeting had been to outline "the method of procedure in the business likely to come before the Board."[3]

Council was in agreement with Ross's suggestion:

> Moved by Alderman L.A. Hamilton seconded by Alderman Coldwell that the Mayor be authorized to forward a petition to the Dominion Government . . . praying that the whole of that part of the Coal Harbor Peninsula known as the Government Reserve or such part as in the wisdom of the Government they might see fit to grant, be conveyed to the City of Vancouver for a Public Park. Carried.[4]

Imagine those men if you can, fifteen or so of them, some bearded, some clean-shaven, dressed in heavy woollen suits, sitting around a long table in a small sitting room in Vancouver's first courthouse, on Water Street, just around the corner from Carrall Street.[5] They were in the original Customs House, with four small prison cells along the inside wall. The junction of Water Street, Carrall Street, Alexander Street, and Powell Street had been the centre of Gastown (Vancouver's predecessor) before it became the centre of the new City of Vancouver. That centre was very close to the natural harbour of Burrard Inlet. It is the corner where Gassy Jack's statue now watches the parade of cars driving through the Gastown neighbourhood.

The petition the council sent to the Dominion Government in Eastern Canada was met with agreement, and on June 8, 1887, thirteen months after sending the request, Vancouver received word that the military reserve on the peninsula could be converted to a city park.

A First Nations trail looped around much of the park peninsula, providing a view of the ocean to the east, the north, and the south, sometimes near the shore, sometimes from a nearby height of land. Work on widening and grading this trail—which the council called Park Road[6]—began shortly after. The existence of a Coast Salish village with a longhouse, and some smaller houses at Whoi Whoi—in an area later called Lumberman's Arch—was ignored. The 8-foot-deep (2.4 metres) midden of shells that had accumulated there over hundreds, possibly thousands, of years was dug up to surface the new road.

Only when Charles Hill-Tout moved from England to Vancouver in the 1890s and became well acquainted with Indigenous

Memorial arch, built to welcome Lord Stanley and his
family in 1889 to the park named for him.

locals was it appreciated that those "shells" represented an archaeological find that was lost forever. Although Hill-Tout was an amateur anthropologist, he would be elected to the Royal Society of Canada in 1913 and would become president of its anthropological section, as well as a fellow of the Royal Anthropological Institute of Great Britain.[7]

The first Park Board committee meeting was held at 4:00 PM on September 26, 1888, at City Hall. The park commissioners were named: A.G. Ferguson (Chairman), R.H. Alexander, Sam Brighouse, Charles A. Coldwell, H.P. McCraney, and R.G. Tatlow.[8]

Next, city council planned a park dedication.

Charles Hilliar was the contractor hired in 1889 to build an arch to welcome Canada's sixth Governor General, Lord Frederick Arthur Stanley of Preston, after whom the park was named. Three young men assisted Hilliar: J.H. Bowman, Will Horrie, and Ed Baynes (later, Vancouver Park Board commissioner from 1924 to 1938). Many years later, Bowman described the construction of this arch in a letter to Major Matthews.

Our work consisted of erecting this memorial arch with the name Stanley Park subscribed thereon. It was erected upon two large cedar logs about 10 ft. high by four or five ft. in diameter placed one on each side of the causeway. The two towers or uprights on these logs being built of 2 × 4 studding about three ft. square by about fifteen or so ft. high, which in turn was close boarded and treated by an ornamental rustication of small cedar poles cut and nailed on horizontally all the way up, between which the arch was sprung or formed and upon which the lettering forming the words "Stanley Park" were cut out of round small cedar poles and nailed to place.

And here is where I must pause a little and toot my own horn. I was very proud of this lettering as I had cut and formed them and always felt they were of right shape and good proportion. The towers on each side were further treated on top with cedar poles pyramid shape and two small flag poles, to which of course flags were flown.

This arch stood for a number of years at the entrance of the park and was considered quite an ornamental rustic feature, but which of course due to time and traffic considerations had to be finally taken down to make way for things of a larger concept.[9]

On October 26, 1889, Lord Stanley and his wife and family arrived in Vancouver by train for the dedication of Stanley Park. Lavish festoons of greenery adorned the engine of the CPR train that carried him west.

Major Matthews later described Lord Stanley's arrival at the park.

(O)n October 29th [1889], Lord Stanley, Governor General, in his carriage drawn by four white horses, passed through the forest then standing on our now populous "West End," and on to Chaythoos, a grassy spot, formerly the site of an Indian village near Prospect Point. There, upon a tiny platform, with arms upraised as though embracing the whole primeval solitude, he dedicated it, "To the use and enjoyment of peoples of all colours, creeds, and customs, for all time."

Then, as he poured the sparkling wine upon the virgin earth, he solemnly declared, "I name thee 'Stanley Park.'"

Stanley Park has changed in size. It originally measured under a thousand acres; it grew to a thousand acres when the Park Board purchased small pieces of adjoining land where the park abutted the city. And then, when Canada went metric in the 1970s, its measurement was stated as four hundred hectares, though that is in fact 988.422 acres. Close enough!

The park has enjoyed some stunning landmark moments. In 1988, a century after being opened and named, it became a National Historic Site of Canada.[10] Each year, Stanley Park welcomes more than 8 million visitors from around the world. In the summer of 2013, *Travel + Leisure* magazine ranked Stanley Park second among the world's twenty-eight most beautiful city parks, citing its skyline views and its forest of a half million western redcedar, Douglas-fir, fir, and western hemlock trees. In 2014, Stanley Park did even better—TripAdvisor named Vancouver's jewel the best park in the world.[11]

From the borders of Stanley Park, many events can be viewed: fireworks in English Bay and Coal Harbour, the Pride Parade, many races, and a polar bear swim every New Year's Day. And inside the park, no matter when you visit, there will always be something going on: a tree-climbing competition; a film shoot; an outdoor wedding with a string quartet; a Big Elf Run; a Terry Fox run; an open-air movie on Ceperley Field; a musical at Theatre Under the Stars; an Easter, Halloween, or Christmas train ride; a concert or a cricket match in Brockton Field; a drumming circle on Third Beach; dancing on Ceperley Playground's basketball court; parades and festivals; horse-drawn carriage rides; and a sale of paintings.

Throughout the year, Vancouver Park Board gardeners and grounds staff maintain the park in excellent shape.

Though you might come for the events, you'll come back for the trees.

2

Beginnings

*We passed to the northward of an island … lying exactly across the canal …
with a smaller island lying before it. From these islands, the canal, in
width about half a mile, continued its directions about east. Here we
were met by about fifty Indians, in their canoes, who conducted themselves with the greatest decorum, and civility, presenting us with several
fish cooked, and undressed, of the sort … resembling the smelt.*

Captain George Vancouver's journal entry of Wednesday, June 13, 1792.
FROM *A VOYAGE OF DISCOVERY*

A Tree Begins Life as a Sapling

THE TIDE MUST have been high when Captain George Vancouver
voyaged here in 1792, giving him the impression that the peninsula
we call Stanley Park was an island. The small island lying before it
was known as Deadman's Island in the park's early years; it is now
HMCS *Discovery*, a branch of the Royal Canadian Navy.

Some of the tree species in Stanley Park today are the same
species Captain Vancouver would have seen all those years ago. To
learn about the park's trees, I realized I would need to refresh my
memory of how fertilization and photosynthesis function. I also
wanted to read the latest and greatest books on tree life, such as
Peter Wohlleben's *The Hidden Life of Trees* and David Suzuki's *Tree*.

In nature, a fertilized tree seed sprouts where it falls to earth.
If it has a hard shell around it (think of a walnut shell), that shell
softens as it moistens on the earth floor. That softening process
might take a long time, a time of vulnerability, when other creatures

Young trees get their start in the shade of an established grove.

might plunder the potential of the seed for themselves.

Eventually, some tree seeds start to emerge from their shells; the miniature roots and shoots start reaching out. Each seedling roots down where it finds itself, seeking out water and a symbiotic relationship with the fungi in the local soil that will supply the tree with the minerals it needs to flourish.

As the seedling secures its foothold down in the earth, it grows a slender stem upward, one that will eventually become a sturdy trunk. The main stem buds and bulges and sends out smaller side stems; leaves unfurl from the buds one by one. The main stem grows taller, tall enough for the young sapling's leaves to reach some sunlight.

Chlorophyll (Greek for "green" and "leaf") in the leaves and stems of the tree captures the sun's energy. This is why leaves are often greener on the side facing the sun and paler on their underside. Through photosynthesis (Greek for "putting something together from light"), chlorophyll combines carbon dioxide and water to create the building blocks of growth and maintenance: sugars, enzymes, and more chlorophyll. The sugar takes simple forms (glucose) and complex forms (starch and cellulose). In the process, it releases some of the extra oxygen from the breakdown of the water molecules.

Around and above our little sapling are its parents and maybe even its grandparents, mature trees of the same species. These far older beings overshadow their offspring, hogging the sunshine, keeping the youngsters from getting too leggy, making the saplings work for their time in the sun.

The roots of the senior members of the forest will communicate and entangle with the sapling's roots, at times sharing nourishment with them. The leaves of neighbouring trees will emit warning scents when danger from pests is imminent. It may be years, a decade, even many decades, before the senior generations are ready to slow down their growth and give up their dominance of the skies. Then the young tree will be strong enough to withstand the winds and rains in the open, above the canopy.

A Human Begins Life as a Baby

At conception, semen (a fluid holding "seeds" in suspension) from a human male fertilizes an ovum ("egg") inside a human female. Many such seeds move out into the world, though it takes only one sperm to unite with one egg to create a human fetus. The fertilized egg begins to grow into a human fetus through cell division and differentiation, developing organs and limbs. In nine months, give or take, the human baby is ready to be born. This was my story. This was your story.

As with the young sapling in the forest, it is many years before a baby grows up. It passes through many stages—newborn, infant, toddler, child, tween, and teen. Maturing continues through the next decades, with a teen finally becoming an adult, and moving away from home to start life on his or her own, to train as something, to start a career, to find a mate, to settle down, and to have a family.

The procreative process continues.

The process of preparing the soil, planting the seed, and waiting for the harvest is a good analogy of the way many people proceed with their careers—training, toiling, applying, and eventually finding themselves in the right place at the right time. By chance. Or by universe.

A forest like the one in Stanley Park—one that has been *somewhat* left to itself—is a beneficial community.

3

Native Trees

The way a crow
Shook down on me
The dust of snow
From a hemlock tree

Has given my heart
A change of mood
And saved some part
Of a day I had rued.

"Dust of Snow," Robert Frost

I Feel Calm and Centred

I FEEL CALM, centred, and connected in a forest. Grounded and present. I feel like that in Stanley Park. Maybe it's because the change in a forest is constant yet unobservable, unobtrusive. Maybe it's because I, as a human being, am so insignificant in size compared with the giants around me. Or because I, as a human being, have lived for such a short time compared with the ancient living beings around me. Or the green and the tree pheromones are so calming.

Whatever the reason, when I am in a forest, I feel calm, centred, and connected. Grounded and present.

I used to feel this way when I skied downhill and when I breast-fed my babies. I feel this way when I stand in the ocean and await the next wave and the next. I feel this way with my grandchildren.

◀ OPPOSITE Winter on the seawall.

That's what being in a forest does for us humans—it calms, centres, and connects us. It brings us to the present moment. That's the gift.

What's That Tree?

All of this centring happens before my analytical left brain kicks in and asks, "What's that tree? Is that bush native to BC? Is that berry safe to eat? What's that bird? How tall is that conifer? What kind of deciduous tree is that?"

Setting myself the task of learning about the trees growing in Stanley Park, I turned to some of the many books written on trees native to this coastal corner of BC, such as *Plants of Coastal British Columbia* by Jim Pojar. I wondered how I would ever get my head around this new subject.

I'm not a botanist, though I did well in my high school botany classes. Our teacher, Miss Taylor, had us carefully sketch the leaves, seeds, and flowers of different plants. But that was all decades ago. I don't remember learning words like *monoecious*, *gymnosperm*, and *angiosperm*. What do they mean? That's why I signed up for Douglas Justice's Fall 2018 "Trees and Shrubs in Landscape" course at the University of British Columbia.

I did learn Latin in high school, and that's proving useful because scientific words can be broken down into their origins, whether Greek or Latin. The word *gymnosperm* reminds me of gymnastics and seeds. Well, in the days of the original Olympics, men always practised their sports naked. And that's what *gymno* means—naked, bare. So the gymnosperms are those plants that release their seeds in a naked form, not in a fleshy fruit with a nut inside. All conifers are gymnosperms.

Okay, good to know.

I'm a student of botany because I'm forever reminding myself of the parts of plants—bracts, stamens, root tip, central vein. If I were a *working* botanist, I would specialize in the processes of decomposition and regeneration that take place in natural forests. Those complex processes have me standing in awe in this muted space. Over and under and within every woody, green, and growing thing is constant symbiosis, silent communication, mutual benefit. Mosses and lichens cover every long-fallen tree branch, and standing ones too. Small ferns grow along the lower branches of mature deciduous trees. Liverworts and algae find toeholds in older living things.

I have not been trained in the art and science of planting, caring for, and maintaining individual trees, so I am definitely not an arborist. Nor do I want to be.

What I am is a tree enthusiast with quite a bit of botanical knowledge who is learning to differentiate between one coniferous tree and another, and between one deciduous tree and another. And I am using more than my eyes. For instance, spruce needles feel sharp. The undersides of many rhododendrons feel velvety and soft. A coast Douglas-fir (*Pseudotsuga menziesii* var. *menziesii*, distinct from the Rocky Mountain Douglas-fir of BC's Interior, var. *glauca*) smells different from a western redcedar. Cottonwood leaves blowing in the wind sound more crackly than the leaves of poplars and aspens, trees in the same genus. And a kousa dogwood fruit tastes sweeter and the texture is mushier (when ripe) than a crabapple.

Many trees can be identified mostly by sight, however. After carrying David Tracey's *Vancouver Tree Book* with me for at least a year whenever I went into the park, I can tell the difference between

A bigleaf maple in the Shakespeare Garden.

1. Trees with leaves that are needles growing in bunches, such as Atlas cedar, western larch, and pines,
2. Trees with leaves that are needles growing singly, such as Douglas-fir and dawn redwood, and
3. Trees with leaves that are overlapping scales, such as western redcedar, cypress, and giant sequoia.

And that only touches on trees with needles or scales. I've learned that trees of the first group (with leaves that are needles growing in bunches) can start to be identified by how many needles are in the bunch.

Where are you on this scale of botanist–tree enthusiast–arborist? How would you describe yourself, tree-wise or knowledge-wise?

In *Tree Book: Learning to Recognize Trees of British Columbia* (a provincial and federal government collaboration), the drawings and descriptions on pages 12 to 15 illustrate the differences between trees with similar features.[1] I use my meagre identification skills to match the monarch I'm standing below with the possible trees on the page. If the needles are too high to see, I look on the ground for cones, no matter the season; there's always some evidence of scattered seeds and leaves. The bark—thick or thin, grooved or smooth—can be a giveaway too.

Western Hemlock

Western hemlock (*Tsuga heterophylla*) is "the most dominant tree in our local forests; it indicates to us that we are in the Coastal Western Hemlock Biogeoclimatic Zone."[2] This evergreen conifer likes to grow from seed by burying itself into the top of a stump, which then becomes a *nurse log*, whose slowly decomposing wood provides nourishment to the seedling as it grows into a tree. Western hemlock grows especially well on nurse logs and thereby dominates the *climax forest* (the forest once it reaches a steady state) in this region. It chases everything else off its territory by growing opportunistically on decaying woody matter before any other tree seeds can get started, by not requiring much sunlight to get started, and by even-

Western hemlock cones.

tually providing such deep shade that other plants are discouraged from growing. And as it establishes itself, growing its roots through, over, and around the stump the seed landed on—the sapling's soil—it gradually consumes, absorbs, and converts all the decomposing nourishment it grows on. (I write more about how a dying tree feeds others in a section in chapter 8 called "Living and Dying." Trees really share the wealth. We can learn a lot from them.)

An older hemlock can resemble an octopus standing on all eight legs, though some will be thick and some will be thin. The "legs" are the roots the tree sends down to the forest floor. The hollowed-out areas show where its benefactor used to be. It grows to be tall (30 to 50 metres) and slender. It's a rather feathery evergreen conifer with drooping top branches, skyward-pointing lower branches, and soft, single needles of different lengths (*hetero* means "different" and *phylla* means "leaves") growing in a flattened spray.

There is an interesting example of a hemlock's growth style east of Pipeline Road and south of the Rose Garden (latitude 49.2981 N | longitude 123.1357 W; see photo on the next page). According to Stacy, one of the Park Board gardeners, this hemlock's drooping top leader broke off at some point, which is why its crown looks atypical for a western hemlock. This tree is interesting because it stands on four bulky legs and several other flimsy ones. It grew from seed as a tiny sapling on top of tall, woody debris. Was that debris a root wad? A nurse log? A slim stump? Whatever provided its soil and nourishment, this hemlock sent roots down into the earth from where it grew on its predecessor, and now it stands on four legs, having consumed all the available nourishment. At the same time that it reached down to the soil, this hemlock also reached up to the sky.

That giant is now beloved of sky.

Western hemlock is one of the three most prolific coniferous trees in the coastal temperate rainforest of Stanley Park. Because western hemlocks grow in thick stands of conifers with other western hemlocks, western redcedars, and Douglas-firs, it's helpful to have lots of ways to identify them. The tree may be too tall and its stand too crowded to discern it from a distance. Its first branches may be too high to see its needles. The bark on a trunk that's as wide as a welcoming embrace has already started to become grooved with age, often with a rather rectangular mosaic look.

The way a western hemlock absorbs the nurse log it grows on is easy to see in this tree that's not in a forest.

I learned a charming Pacific Northwest Indigenous tale about western hemlocks when I went on a Stanley Park Ecology Society walk. This tale helps me identify western hemlocks. One day, Mother Nature called together all the evergreen trees in the forest. She told them she was going to give them cones, and pointed to a large pile of cones of different sizes. The hemlock, believing himself to be the tallest and, therefore, the most important tree in the forest, elbowed himself to the front of the line. Mother Nature was shocked at his boldness. She sent him to the back of the line and began handing out cones of various shapes and lengths and weights.

After a while, the hemlock decided it must be his turn now. He elbowed himself to the front of the line once more. Again, he was sent to the back.

The line went on all day like this, from sunrise to sunset.

Finally, as the sun began to dip into the horizon, it was Hemlock's turn.

"From this day forth," proclaimed Mother Nature, "you shall bow your head in shame for having been so proud." And she handed Hemlock a very small cone, no bigger than a man's thumbnail.

Hemlock returned to the forest and tried to grow up to the sky, like the tallest trees around him, but no matter how hard he tried, he would always bow his head in shame.

The moral of the story—as they used to say—is be confident but not proud, forthright but not pushy.

More Evergreens

The other two most prolific conifers in Stanley Park are western redcedars and Douglas-firs.

BC's official tree is the western redcedar, an evergreen that is ubiquitous along the Pacific coastline. With its vertically lined bark, gracefully drooping shape (often with branches that touch the ground), overlapping shiny green scales, sprays of small woody cones (the size of a pinkie nail), and aroma, it is the easiest conifer to recognize.

The scientific name for western redcedars is *Thuja plicata*. *Plicata* refers to the plaited—braided—nature of its small leaves, growing in flat sprays. *Thuja* is the name in Greek mythology of a river nymph, a sprite who was the first to offer sacrifices to Dionysus, the god of the harvest. The name *Thuja* was given in 1753 by the Swedish botanist Carl Linnaeus to this genus of trees within the cypress family.

Coast Salish Peoples know the western redcedar as "the tree of life," because it has supplied them with clothing, basket-making material, tools, construction material, medicines, and tea. And indeed, thujas are also commonly called *arborvitae*, Latin for "tree of life."

I find it easy to identify western redcedar trees. For a start, they exude that cedar smell—sweet, warm, and relaxing. The reddish bark grows in vertical, fibrous strips, making it easy for Indigenous people to harvest it for ropes and mats. A western redcedar grows branches of overlapping fronds of scaled leaves that hang down low to the ground. Its cones group together in clusters on the sprays of scaled leaves, their appearance changing from little oval green berries to little oval brown woody cones. They are among the smallest cones in this forest. And as it happens, western redcedars have much smaller cones than hemlocks—about half the size.

The way to differentiate between a western redcedar and a cypress, or a false cypress, is to look for the cones: the redcedar's female cones are oval, whereas the cypress's are round, like a miniature soccer ball.

The Latin name for a Douglas-fir is *Pseudotsuga menziesii* (more about its name in chapter 5). A Douglas-fir has a massive trunk with bark so thick and furrowed that small mammals are able to hide inside it during forest fires; its corky bark doesn't burn and the animals stay safe. That feature leads us to recognize its cones: they sport tridentate scales (*tridentate* translates as "three teeth") that protect the seeds, and these scales have been interpreted in another Pacific Northwest Indigenous myth as the little tail and hind paws of a deer mouse—a mouse hiding inside the Douglas-fir's grooved bark. Once you recognize this feature of a Douglas-fir cone, you'll never forget it. The cones are 6 to 9 centimetres long, and they fall intact to the forest floor. The flat, single needles of a Douglas-fir are spirally arranged, giving the effect of a sometimes-spindly green bottle brush. The needle tips are either sharp or blunt, but not prickly.

Stanley Park is only a *fairly* natural forest. It is not pristine. After all, it was logged by six small companies as early as the 1860s and well into the 1890s. And these companies particularly logged the Douglas-fir trees.

In addition, after weather disasters brought down Stanley Park trees by the thousands, the provincial government of BC stepped in and removed fallen trees. In February 1935, the minutes of a Vancouver Park Board meeting recorded, "Severe

ABOVE Western redcedar (*Thuja plicata*) needles and cones.

LEFT Heavy crop of immature cones on western redcedar.

Male pollen cones on a young grand fir (*Abies grandis*).

trees in the forest. In addition to planting Douglas-firs and western redcedars, they planted Sitka spruce (*Picea sitchensis*) and grand firs (*Abies grandis*). The Sitka spruce is a dense conifer that exhibits the typical Christmas-tree shape. It grows long cones (5 to 10 centimetres) that hang down and have a unique honeycomb appearance. Its needles are arranged spirally around a central stem and they have a sharp point. Sitka spruce is robust in its native Alaska but has not always fared well in Stanley Park, and as a result, many specimens have been cut back.

Grand firs live up to their name, growing up to 25 metres tall (taller than the Sitka spruce) by the time they're around forty-five years old. Their spread is up to 10 metres, and they also display the Christmas-tree shape, with soft-tipped needles. True firs grow their female cones high in the crown of the tree; the cones release their seeds bit by bit as they mature. So, unlike finding cones in the duff around a Douglas-fir, it's impossible to find a female grand fir cone on the ground. The male cones are easier to see in lower branches, waiting for wind to waft their pollen through the forest.

Once in a while in Stanley Park's forest, I come across a Pacific yew (*Taxus brevifolia*), another native conifer. Its gentle needles are soft, swaying with the slightest breeze.

storm has hit city; damage in Stanley Park so great that Provincial Attorney General has visited site and provides $20,000 worth of Relief labour to clear downed trees."[3] The "severe storm" had happened in 1934 and was called for years thereafter the "Great Storm."

After later storms (and even during mild weather, for other reasons), Park Board employees have planted native BC

Deciduous or Angiosperm

I used to separate trees into two groups: evergreen and deciduous. But now I realize how misleading that is. *Deciduous* is from the Latin *decidere*, meaning "to fall off." The word *deciduous* has come to refer to trees whose leaves fall off every autumn, or at least before winter. However, the leaves of all trees do eventually fall off at the end of their life span—a process termed *senescence*. But since an evergreen tree or shrub takes up to seven years to renew all its leaves irregularly, it has the appearance of being forever green.

Now I know that better terms for dividing trees into two groups (as though that were truly possible) are *gymnosperm* ("with naked seeds") and *angiosperm* ("with seeds in a receptacle"). In medical terminology, *angio* also refers to receptacles: blood vessels and the heart. Think of the word *angiogram*, the x-ray used for blood vessels and the heart, to remember the term. Because a seed forms in a gymnosperm when male pollen fertilizes female ovaries, gymnosperm trees need wind to blow the male sperms against the female eggs. They require the elements of wind and water to spread their fertilized seed, and some of them require the element of fire to prepare suitable soil for the seed to grow in (such as Douglas-firs).

Some angiosperms rely on wind, but many more rely on insects, birds, and small mammals to assist with their procreation and spread. They use various means of attracting creatures, including scent and colour. Think of the honeybee flying from flower to flower, gathering nectar to feed her colony's young, and picking up pollen from the flowers en route. Or the burrs that attach to a dog or raccoon's underbelly when it walks through a forest.

One other way to describe angiosperms is as broadleaf species. In other words, their leaves are not needles.

Northern black cottonwood *(Populus trichocarpa)* at Lumberman's Arch.

Northern black cottonwood (*Populus trichocarpa*), red alder (*Alnus rubra*), and bigleaf maple (*Acer macrophyllum*) are the most prolific native deciduous trees in Stanley Park. There's a beauty of a cottonwood growing alone in the open to the west of the curved avenue of London plane trees above Lumberman's Arch; its lower trunk is covered with suckers. Bigleaf maples, with their platter-sized leaves (40 centimetres across—larger than a man's hand) comprising five deep lobes, are easy to recognize.

Red alders sprout up wherever there's an opportunity in the open; they love sunlight. They benefit the soil by fixing nitrogen in previously infertile soil. There are fewer of them in the forested areas of the park. Their deep green leaves are oval, roughly toothed, with 8 to 15 veins coming off the central vein. What helps me differentiate them from cottonwood leaves is that the side veins of red alder leaves are deeply grooved, growing straight and parallel to each other and ending in a bigger tooth. A cottonwood leaf, on the other hand, is more heart shaped, its

resin smells slightly bitter, and it turns brown as it dries. Its side veins are curved, and the leaf edge sports only insignificant teeth.

Native to BC, the Pacific dogwood (*Cornus nuttallii*) is the province's flower emblem. Dogwood is at its most gorgeous in full bloom, studded overall with intricate white or pink blossoms of between 4 and 8 petals (technically *bracts*) that surround the minute central flowers.

Sometimes I'll see an arbutus (*Arbutus menziesii*), its identity given away by peeling bark that exposes a smooth, khaki-coloured trunk and branches.

As our summers get hotter, drier, and longer with climate change (already indi-cated in recent summers), arbutus may be one of several trees native to this province that are now being planted here in the park more often.

These many gymnosperm and angio-sperm trees can be seen all around the seawall, along the trails, and edging every carefully manicured space. They've also been planted within the park's several gardens.

Previously, all I saw when I walked in the park was trees. Now I'm starting to recognize my friends, Douglas-firs, western hemlocks, western redcedars, red alders, and bigleaf maples. How about you? How many friends do you recognize?

4

Timber!

*Lumbermen in their winter camp, daybreak in the woods, stripes of
snow on the limbs of trees, the occasional snapping . . .*

Leaves of Grass, Walt Whitman

INDIGENOUS PEOPLE HAVE many uses for the bark of western
redcedar. They peel off strips of the fibrous red bark in the spring
when the sap is running. Traditionally, the women would wet it and
roll it in their hands to make rope of various thicknesses and lengths,
and fabric for weaving and matting.

When Indigenous people wanted to fell a cedar tree—to make a
dugout canoe or a totem pole or a house, or cedar shakes for a house or
for serving platters or for a slab for sliding down frozen rivers—they first
established whether the tree was rotten inside. Using a stone chisel and
a big round stone for a hammer, they would cut an exploratory hole a few
feet up the trunk to find out if the tree was sound. If they struck a rotten
centre, they abandoned the tree and looked for another suitable tree.[1]

Dugout canoes had two purposes. Either they were for navigat-
ing the ocean waters around the peninsula and into the harbour, or
they were for ceremonial burial use. It was believed that deceased
loved ones would have a faster passage home if their bodies were put
in a dugout canoe high up a tree. This also kept the bodies safe from
coyotes (still in the park today) and bears (long gone).

Major James Skitt Matthews, Vancouver's first city archivist,
became good friends with a Squamish man named August Jack

Khahtsahlano. August was the son of Khay-Tulk (also known as Supplejack) of the Capilano Indian Reserve, and the grandson of Chief Khahtsahlano, from whom the neighbourhood of Kitsilano takes its name. In July 1943, Matthews asked August how an Indigenous man would fell a tree with a stone hammer and stone chisel. Matthews learned that the procedure was complicated, and he rewrote it in a way he could understand after the interview was over. As he often did, Major Matthews signed and dated his interview and had the interviewee approve it for accuracy.

> Mr. Khahtsahlano . . . shows in his drawing that, after a suitable tree [one that was already leaning] was selected, a cut was put in, severing the trunk to a depth of about half way through or more. Wedges were then driven in at a point where the cut was deepest, on both sides of the trunk, with the result that, due to the weight of the leaning trunk on the uncut portion of the tree, assisted by the force of the wedges in creating the commencement of a split, the split ultimately ran up the trunk and this caused the half which had been cut through to swing out, at the bottom, and the top of the tree to lean still more until finally, it toppled over . . . At the conclusion of the operation, the log lay on the ground with most of the branches of the tree still attached, and the uncut por-

tion still stood upright as a tapering spike broken at the top.

Matthews asked how long the procedure would take, and how long it took to carve the log into a canoe.

> Maybe one man one month . . . if he works every day from daylight to sunset. No eight hours in those Indian days . . .
>
> When the canoe made, take it to the beach; not take the log to the beach. No horse, no mule, all hand power.[2]

August must have been describing a very simple canoe, for when Major Matthews interviewed Noel Robinson, a member of the Canadian Legion, West End Branch, he learned it could take up to one or two years to make a canoe.[3]

For several decades before Stanley Park officially became a park, and for quite a while after, small western logging outfits selectively logged some of the bigger Douglas-firs and western redcedars within its forest, to market as ship masts, or spars. The loggers used the springboard system, creating a ledge to hold a board at about shoulder height, which two men could stand on, one on each end. This allowed them to use heavy

▶ OPPOSITE Loggers use the springboard system to fell a massive Douglas-fir.

RIGHT Loggers use the springboard system to fell another Douglas-fir.

BELOW Selective logging in Stanley Park took place into the 1890s.

double-edged axes, taking turns to chop into the massive trunk; alternatively, they sawed back and forth with long two-handled saws.

Loggers then hauled out the timber using teams of massive oxen or draft horses, pulling the logs in a long train over "corduroy roads," also known as "skid roads," which were trails made of small felled logs laid at right angles.

What damage each tree must have caused to the undergrowth as it fell! I can only imagine the reverberations and the broken saplings in the understorey. The previously silent climax forest would have shaken and rippled and swayed with the crash. Small and large animals would have leapt and scurried away. Small winged creatures would have flown off.

One of the bigger logging outfits was run by English mariner and businessman Edward Stamp, who began his logging and milling operations at Brockton Point, through the company he had formed in 1865: the British Columbia and Vancouver Island Spar, Lumber, and Saw Mill Company. With permission to log much of the area that is now Vancouver, Stamp planned first to fell all the large trees in the government reserve and mill them into timber. This was before the government reserve on the peninsula had been declared a park.

The manufacturers of milling machinery in Glasgow neglected to send some of Captain Stamp's order, with the result that he didn't begin logging until 1867. In the meantime, he employed loggers to fell the bigger trees, and using teams of horses and oxen, he had the logs hauled to Coal Harbour. He created a log boom to hold the logs just offshore at Brockton Point, but he soon found that the rapid ocean currents and a nearby reef made it an inconvenient location.

Apparently, Stamp had a difficult personality. He fell out with his principal backers and was let go from his management position. The company went into liquidation and was sold for ten cents on the dollar, then moved to what became known as Hastings Mill on the eastern shore of Coal Harbour.

This mill became the basis, the foundation, the beginnings, of the settlement of Gastown, the precursor to Vancouver. But for ocean currents, a nearby reef, an incomplete delivery of milling equipment, and Captain Stamp's difficult personality, Vancouver might have grown up on what became Stanley Park, rather than around the Hastings Mill location at the foot of Dunlevy Avenue.

The future Stanley Park had been spared.

Walking along Stanley Park's trails at various times, I have seen almost every kind of evidence of early logging: tall stumps that display saw marks, axe marks, and square holes, and still-standing trees that display round holes—the trees that were abandoned because they were deemed unsuitable, perhaps because they had a rotten centre. There

A team of oxen hauls logs over a corduroy trail.

is one gigantic Douglas-fir whose marks suggest it was considered by non-Indigenous loggers and then abandoned, perhaps because they noticed it housed a bald eagle's aerie. That Douglas-fir is at the corner of Tatlow Walk and Bridle Path (see page 4 for its photo).

What I haven't noticed is a live tree pointing skyward like a spike, or a snag (a still-standing dead tree)—the remains of a tree that was half-harvested for an Indigenous canoe. I must look more carefully. Let me know if you see one, though maybe too much time has passed since the last one was felled that way.

5

The First Primitive Crossing

Early on the Morning of the 12th, Capt. Vancouver set off in the Pinnace
accompanied by Lieut. Puget in the Launch to explore the Shore &
openings on the North side of the great North West Arm. These Boats
were well armed & equipped with every necessary for 10 days.

Archibald Menzies's journal entry of June 12, 1792, while anchored at Birch Bay,
Washington. From *Menzies' Journal of Vancouver's Voyage.*

WHEN CAPTAIN GEORGE Vancouver was exploring what would become Burrard Inlet, he might have seen one very particular Douglas-fir growing taller than its neighbours. The geography of this southwest corner of what would be mainland British Columbia was very much like it is today. The inhabitants were Coast Salish peoples—the Squamish, the Musqueam, and the Tsleil-Waututh Nations. The buildings, the businesses, and the hustle and bustle that make up present-day Vancouver were absent.

There was, however, one very old, very tall, very particular Douglas-fir—particular because of its location.

Douglas-firs are best named with a hyphen because they're not true fir trees. Their Latin name is *Pseudotsuga menziesii*, which means they are pseudo-hemlocks, so they're not true hemlocks either. But they are in the Pinaceae or cone-bearing pine family of pines, firs, hemlocks, cedars, larches, and spruces—all trees that bear needles singly or in bunches on the stem (rather than as sprays of overlapping scales, as in a western redcedar, for instance).

◀ OPPOSITE Evening light fades as an empty cargo ship enters Burrard Inlet to load up at the Port of Vancouver.

Snow melts from noble fir needles in mid-December.

Pseudo-hemlocks, Douglas-firs, were first discovered and their seed collected by Archibald Menzies, the Scottish surgeon, botanist, and naturalist who travelled with Captain George Vancouver on his 1792 voyage to the west coast of North America. This was the voyage during which Vancouver entered Burrard Inlet and met with Coast Salish First Nations. Menzies was appointed by Sir Joseph Banks to preserve "such new or uncommon plants as he might deem worthy of a place amongst His Majesty's very valuable collection of exotics at Kew."[1]

In those days, young men who trained as surgeons received an education that included botany; naval surgeons were hired as travelling apothecaries who could both perform a leg amputation and advise on the best choice of tall evergreen for brewing the fresh batches of beer that protected sailors from scurvy. With experience of the chronic constipation that plagued ocean-going explorers, Menzies was also on the lookout for fruit as he botanized on shore.

Two new species of *Vaccinium* [*V. parvifolium* and *ovalifolium* (Red and Black Huckleberry)] was pretty common in the woods & grew in some places to upwards of 12 feet high, the one had large black berries & the other red, which were now beginning to ripen, & as they posessd a gratefull acidity we found them extremely pleasant & palatable after being so long upon salt provision. The only other fruit which the woods at this time afforded us was a new species of Rasberry that grew at least to ten feet high, & of which there were two varieties, one with a large red fruit & another with a yellow that were both equally gratefull & pleasant but were not met with in any great abundance. These Fruits together with a daily supply of fresh Spruce Beer greatly assisted to correct the bad tendency of our present mode of living.[2]

Because Menzies was the first European to identify and collect Douglas-firs, their Latin name includes his: *menziesii*. The common or garden name for Douglas-firs, however, pays tribute to another Scottish botanist, David Douglas, a young naturalist whom Menzies met and mentored in the 1820s when Menzies returned to England for the last time and Douglas set out for the west for the first time.[3] In 1828, Douglas described some of the forest trees he considered had a great future. Of the Douglas-fir, he wrote,

> The wood may be found very useful for a variety of domestic purposes: the young slender ones exceedingly well adapted for making ladders and scaffold poles, not being liable to cast; the larger timber for more important purposes; while at the same time the rosin may be found deserving attention.[4]

In listing in his journal those plants that David Douglas introduced into Great Britain during the years 1826 to 1834, Douglas does not mention *Pseudotsuga menziesii*. That is because he knows that Menzies introduced it. Indeed, Menzies included it in his list of introduced plants as *Pseudotsuga taxifolia*, a species name that was deemed in 1955 to be "illegal" in favour of *Pseudotsuga menziesii*.[5] And yet the species is not listed in *Monkey Puzzle Man: Archibald Menzies, Plant Hunter*,

A foggy day in English Bay.

the best biography of Archibald Menzies that I could find, and it is erroneously added to the lists of trees that David Douglas introduced to Great Britain by some of Douglas's biographers. Ah well. The vagaries of the "truth" in "history," according to who is writing it.

Let me go back to that very old, very tall, very particular Douglas-fir, which was particular because of its location and its age. Perhaps Captain Vancouver saw it when he and his crew travelled east into the inlet—which he named for his friend Sir Harry Burrard—even though it was growing tucked away out of sight to the south, at the narrowest place between the peninsula that would become Stanley Park and the rest of the future Vancouver. The bulk of that peninsula hid it. And besides, there were thousands of other trees around.

That place is near where the sign reading "WELCOME TO VANCOUVER, HOST CITY —2010 OLYMPIC AND PARALYMPIC WINTER GAMES | BIENVENUE À VANCOUVER, VILLE HÔTE—JEUX OLYMPIQUES ET PARALYMPIQUES D'HIVER DE 2010" stands now, and a hundred or so feet northwest of the 0 miles/km marker on the seawall.

Even though there is no longer any physical evidence of this giant, I know it existed, because by 1886, it had fallen and been repurposed. Its new purpose is described in volume two of *Early Vancouver*, a *Narrative of Pioneers of Vancouver* compiled by Major James Skitt Matthews over 1932, one year before he had sufficiently pestered local officials to grant him the position of Vancouver's first archivist.[6]

On June 16, 1932, Major Matthews interviewed a pioneer widow, Mrs. Emily Eldon. She reminisced in detail about her early days living in Vancouver, her memory jogged by the major's questions.

Emily and her first husband, a Scottish builder and handyman by the name of Alexander Strathie (sometimes spelled Straithie), came west from Winnipeg together and spent a year in Victoria. They moved to Vancouver in the spring of 1886, on March 1, to be precise. This was only a few months before a horrendous fire transformed the vibrant young city to ashes.

STANLEY PARK BEFORE "THE FIRE." It had been our custom, my husband's and mine, to take a walk on Sunday afternoons; sometimes, indeed frequently, we went towards the west, along a narrow trail which led from Water Street in the direction of Coal Harbour, and English Bay. The trail led . . . between what is now Pender Street and Seaton Street [Hastings Street West] . . . and wandered on towards what is now the entrance to Stanley Park. It was a narrow track, lined with bushes so thick and close that it was necessary for a woman to draw in her skirts close around her legs to avoid her clothing being torn.

THE FIRST STANLEY PARK "BRIDGE." At almost the exact spot where, first the bridge, and afterwards the present causeway was built, was the narrowest point of Coal Harbour—that was why the bridge was built there—an enormous tree had fallen across Coal Harbour, and its trunk formed the first primitive crossing into our great park, or as we called it then, The Reserve. It was an enormous tree with its roots still attached.

Where it came from I don't know, likely blown over, perhaps drifted in. I never saw such tremendous limbs on a tree. Tree and branches rested in the mud

George and Emily Eldon in front of their park ranger home in Stanley Park.

and water, which, when the tide was in, was fairly deep. I recall how gingerly we crossed the trunk of that tree, and how my husband used to exclaim, "Now, be careful, don't fall into that water."

I was young then, and enjoyed the scramble across the tree trunk; once on the far side we hopped from boulder to boulder till we got to dry land, and then strolled down the skid roads until it was time to go home again.[7]

Sometime after her first husband died, Emily married George Eldon, park ranger of Stanley Park from 1896 to 1903. The couple lived in the park ranger's cottage, which was accessible from the Georgia Street entrance to Stanley Park. On the previous page is a picture of them enjoying their cottage garden that included tulips, hyacinths, and a very young monkey puzzle tree.[8]

In 1904, Eldon became the first superintendent of parks,[9] and in January 1906, a log house was built for him and Emily at 2099 Beach Avenue, the current location of the Vancouver Park Board offices. Once Eldon retired, in 1910, he and his wife moved into town, and the next superintendent and his family moved in at 2099 Beach Avenue.

There is no record in Major Matthews's notes and publications regarding the fate of that very old, very tall, very particular Douglas-fir that fell and settled in a place that allowed it to become the first primitive crossing to the park. But I can see it now in my mind's eye, settled with its "tremendous limbs" into the mud of Coal Harbour, enabling many fit young Vancouverites to make the crossing and walk in the park on a Sunday afternoon, before a bridge was ever constructed.

6

Fire!

Vancouver June 22nd, 1886
a special meeting of the council was held
on Tuesday June 22nd at 3 o'clock PM

Moved by Alderman Northcott seconded by Alderman Cordiner that
Mr. Ronald's Fire Engine be purchased on Condition that he Furnish
us with 2000 feet of the Maltese Cross brand of hose with Couplings
Complete at a price not exceeding 1.25 per foot and that 4 hose reels,
4 nozzles and two branches be added. Carried.

Minutes from the Vancouver City Council meeting in 1886

THE COLLECTION OF businesses, houses, and shacks that garnered the name "Gastown" from its saloonkeeper, Gassy Jack Deighton, owed its existence partly to logging. Gold digging and logging. Gassy Jack garnered his name from his talkative nature.

When the people of Gastown laid out the plan for a townsite, it came to be renamed Granville, after Great Britain's secretary of state for foreign affairs, Granville Leveson-Gower, Second Earl Granville, a man who lived in far-off London. The settlement of Granville took itself more seriously than Gastown did. It still owed its existence to logging—not to the hope of finding gold or coal (which hadn't panned out), but to the actuality of the timber industry—gigantic trees, logging, a sawmill, and lumber.

When the Canadian Pacific Railway acted upon its promise to unite Canada into one country, from Eastern Canada to BC, Granville

Real Estate Office
In Big Tree — Copyright applied for

James Horne, an early landowner in Vancouver, arranged for this posed photograph to advertise his real estate company. Pioneer George Cary told Major Matthews years later that the "Georgia Street tree," as it was known, "was cut up in sections; part went to Queen Victoria's Jubilee Exhibition in London, part to Toronto, and a piece stood on Hastings Street for years."

The men in the photograph from left to right on the ground are Mr. Stiles, A.W. Ross, Dr. Luke Port, J.W. Horne, Mr. Hendrickson, and US Consul Mr. Hemming. Men on the log from left to right are H.A. Jones, Mr. Perry, and an unidentified man thought to be Mr. Perry's partner. The photographer is H.T. Devine.

renamed itself again. It became Vancouver, after Captain George Vancouver, the explorer who first sailed into Burrard Inlet in 1792. The City of Vancouver incorporated its townsite on April 6, 1886. Vancouver owes its existence to its lush rainforest setting, a worldwide market for wood products, a railway link with the east, an ocean route to the Far East, its scenic snow-covered mountains, and the rugged nature of its early settlers, the pioneers. Vancouver was fully aware of being reliant on its trees, and when one of the really huge Douglas-firs in the middle of town fell in May 1886, James Welton Horne quickly took advantage of the advertising opportunity to attract more settlers to his company, J.W. Horne Real Estate.

Two months and one week after its April incorporation, on Sunday, June 13, 1886, the City of Vancouver went up in flames—a fierce, all-consuming fire that left the young city in ashes. The memory of that day and its aftermath burned itself into the minds of all those involved.

It seems that many young cities in Western Canada and the US burned down soon after establishing themselves. Their being built almost entirely out of wood was definitely a factor. But it also seemed to take the scare of a sudden fire to make citizens more careful, and for the city to acquire fire-response equipment and staff. It was the same with Vancouver, and Stanley Park benefited.

In an interview with city archivist Major Matthews forty-five years after the "Great Fire," a real estate broker and alderman on the first city council, William H. Gallagher, described how that conflagration might have started. Gallagher had acted as a special constable the night after the Great Fire, keeping order in the young city.

The men who cut down the forest where now stands the most important business section of our city—that is, roughly from Cambie Street to Burrard Street, north and south between creek and inlet— adopted the expedient of cutting the backs only of the smaller trees, and then let a big tree down upon them; the whole thing would go down with a crash, like a lot of ninepins. After the first attempts at this system were proven successful, they enlarged it, and as the falling progressed southwards towards Davie Street—they had started from Burrard Inlet and worked south—a whole section of ten or more, perhaps twenty acres, would go down with one great grand sweeping crash . . . When the fire came, the Great

TOP A staged grouping of city aldermen for the first City of Vancouver council meeting following the Great Fire of 1886.

BOTTOM Some of Vancouver's fire-prevention measures after the Great Fire of 1886.

One of many fire hydrants in Stanley Park is tucked under a group of western redcedars.

Fire, it was largely through this abundance of slashing fallen earlier in the summer, and very dry, which caused the fire to rage so fiercely . . .

Before I left our camp, the fire had gained such momentum that it was impossible to see the sky; the air was just one mass of fiery flame driven before a strong rising southwest wind . . . The city did not burn; it was consumed by flame; the buildings simply melted before the fiery blast . . .

We converted one of the buildings (on Westminster Avenue) into a morgue, and before daylight had deposited the remains of twenty-one persons there . . . It was the gum and pitch which made the fire so terrible, so fierce, and created a black, bitter smoke more smothering than burning oil.

Rebuilding started the very next day.

The next city council meeting was held in front of a tent. Some of the important items on subsequent meeting agendas were purchasing a fire engine, hiring a fire crew, and establishing fire procedures.

The trees growing on the peninsula of land that was named Stanley Park on September 27, 1888, were untouched by Vancouver's Great Fire. Gradually, in the years to come, when fire hydrants became commonplace on city streets, they were also installed in the park, protecting our heritage from fire. Even though Stanley Park was not touched by the Great Fire, it has been touched by lightning strikes and small fires from dropped matches. One way and another, the park has benefited from the fire-prevention measures that began after the Great Fire of 1886.

7

The Big Fir

The wealth and prosperity of western North America owes much to the Douglas fir. Trees can grow to a thousand years or more in the absence of catastrophic fire, and their thick, corky bark is effective at insulating trees from less intense fires.

Douglas Justice, Vancouver Trees app

ABOUT THREE OR four hundred years before the very tall, very particular Douglas-fir tree fell to create the first primitive crossing to the park, it was a mere seed—a germinated seed falling on fertile soil. Nearby—we'll never now know how near—was another germinated seed. Perhaps the two seeds were from cones off the same tree, or maybe they were from the same previous stand of Douglas-firs.

When the gigantic Douglas-fir that became the first crossing to the peninsula fell, its comrade, a sentinel Douglas-fir that became known as "the big fir," remained standing. Shaken, but still standing.

I can just imagine a nineteenth-century couple—let's call them Harold and Myrtle—arranging a date: "Let's meet by the big fir near the entrance to our great park and go for a walk this Sunday, Myrtle."

"What a refreshing idea, Harold."

Neighbours might say, "Let's gather at the big fir to walk into the park for Sunday's concert at the bandstand."

On page 53 is a beautiful photograph of the big fir as a gathering place in 1906. Notice the mother with her three children, waiting for her husband, clustering around the darkened bole (trunk) of the Douglas-fir.

Georgia Street entrance to Stanley Park in 1894. Notice
"the big fir" on the left of the image.

Also visible in this image is the wooden bridge set on pylons buried deep into the mudflats of Burrard Inlet's Coal Harbour; this is the bridge that replaced the fallen Douglas-fir. That first primitive crossing is long gone.

Just as the fallen Douglas-fir had done before, this bridge provided a link at the narrowest part of Coal Harbour, from Vancouver to the young city's park playground. I have studied this bridge in many old photographs. It was wide enough on the east side for two lanes of horse-drawn and engine-powered vehicles—the west lane going into the park and the east lane coming out. (All traffic in Canada drove on the left until January 1, 1922.) A raised pedestrian path was set to the west of these two driving lanes.

Three strict orders were posted at the park entrance on the temporary archway built to welcome Lord Stanley.

NOTICE. ANY PERSON FOUND SHOOTING OR CUTTING TIMBER OR LIGHTING FIRES WITHIN THIS PARK SHALL BE PROSECUTED ACCORDING TO LAW.

NOTICE. ALL PERSONS DRIVING ALONG THIS BRIDGE ARE REQUIRED NOT TO EXCEED A WALKING PACE.

NO HEAVY WAGONS ALLOWED TO HAUL ON PARK ROAD.

Eventually, cars began taking over from carriages and wagons. In 1905, one year after Canada's automotive industry began with the establishment of the Ford Motor Company of Canada in Eastern Canada, the Park Board received its first formal complaint of "horses taking flight" in Stanley Park when confronted by cars. As

A family waits at "the big fir" in 1906.

Cars at Prospect Point in Stanley Park in 1908.

a temporary measure, the board restricted automobile access to the park until "horses get accustomed to automobiles."[1] In that first decade of the twentieth century, cars in the park made a suitable photograph subject. The picture above was taken at Prospect Point. Nowadays, I try to avoid including a car in my photos.

The bridge to the park was attractive, with its pattern of crossed beams. Midspan was a reinforced section that was open below to allow canoes and rowboats to pass back and forth.

The world over, ocean tides come in and go out, come in and go out, their heights and times influenced by the gravitational forces of the sun and moon, combined with Earth's rotation on its axis. In Vancouver, there are two high tides and two low tides during each twenty-four-hour day. The heights of the

high tides are not identical, and vary from day to day; the same goes for the heights of the low tides. The difference between the lowest low tide and the highest high tide around Vancouver is as much as 3.4 metres (11 feet 2 inches).

In some places, such as English Bay and Second Beach, when the tide goes out, a sandy beach is exposed, inviting locals and tourists alike to beachcomb, sunbathe, build sandcastles, and look for crabs in the remaining rock pools. Much of that sand was brought in, and aren't we glad it was. Here's why. When the tide went out under the wooden bridge that connected Vancouver with Stanley Park, a large mud flat was exposed, part of the open bay of Coal Harbour—to be precise, 16.6 hectares (41 acres) of mud. The people of Vancouver were not impressed. The mud wasn't appealing.

In her charming way, canoer Pauline Johnson named the mud flat to the west of the wooden bridge "Lost Lagoon." Johnson was the daughter of a hereditary Mohawk chief and an Englishwoman who had immigrated with her family to North America as a child.

As a princess-poet, Pauline Johnson travelled North America and the British Isles for fifteen years, giving matinee and evening recitals of her own prose and poetry. She would open her program wearing buckskin and wampum beads and end her performance in a Victorian gown. This legendary

Canadian moved to Vancouver in 1909 and became very familiar with its Indigenous legends and open spaces.

When Coal Harbour's high tide was in, Pauline could paddle her canoe west into the lagoon through the mid-span opening in the bridge. When the tide went out, she couldn't. The name Lost Lagoon stuck; the fact that she published a poem with that title helped.

Lost Lagoon

It is dusk on the Lost Lagoon,
And we two dreaming the dusk away,
Beneath the drift of a twilight grey,
Beneath the drowse of an ending day,
And the curve of a golden moon.

It is dark in the Lost Lagoon,
And gone are the depths of haunting blue,
The grouping gulls, and the old canoe,
The singing firs, and the dusk and you,
And gone is the golden moon.

O! lure of the Lost Lagoon,
I dream to-night that my paddle blurs
The purple shade where the seaweed stirs,
I hear the call of the singing firs
In the hush of the golden moon.

E. Pauline Johnson[2]

The Vancouver Park Board felt they should do something about the muddy eyesore that Pauline Johnson had named so poetically. In 1905, they voted to accept the

The 72nd Seaforth Highlanders of Canada cross the bridge into Stanley Park in 1914.

first major development scheme for Lost Lagoon, which was to fill it in. The only thing stopping the board from carrying out that scheme was a lack of funds.

By 1912, the area had become the subject of a heated debate. Some people wanted to fill in the bay for dry-land sports use, while others wanted to convert it to full-time water use. In 1913, grand plans arose to build an art gallery and museum on the north shore.

The First World War intervened, and many men and some women signed up to fight. The picture of the 72nd Seaforth Highlanders of Canada shows hundreds of men (many of them of Scottish descent) trooping into the park for training at Brockton Point. The regiment was not approved to fight in the First World War until 1916. Notice the "big fir" on the right of the photo.

Progress on the causeway construction by November 1917.

In 1916, the Park Board approved an ambitious plan to replace the wooden bridge to Stanley Park with a wide causeway that would enable heavier wagons and more cars to drive into the park. This causeway would also block the natural to and fro of Coal Harbour's tides. The lagoon area would be pumped full of fresh water, so the originally salty habitat for flora and fauna would have to evolve.

Back to the story of our sentinel Douglas-fir, with its straight bole and horizontal branches of various lengths visible in many early photographs. It can still be seen on the extreme left of this stark panorama taken of the causeway construction with a wide-angle lens in 1917.

Somewhere in 1918 or 1919, the big fir came down, a victim of the causeway's construction. I would rather believe it died of old

age or fell down in a violent wind, and was allowed to release all its woody nutrients back into the ground to nourish the earth once more, like many another ancient member of the forest. But I'm certain that's not what happened.

In *Vancouver Tree Book*, David Tracey writes, "Some Douglas-fir trees have survived more than 1,000 years, overcoming all challenges but dunderheads. The Stanley Park Ecology Society says a venerable 99-m-tall Douglas-fir that used to tower over the entrance to the park was cut down for firewood."[3] Tracey is describing the big fir. Standing in the way of progress, it had to come down.

When the First World War ended, Canadians were eager to relax and enjoy themselves. The new freedom, combined with the wider causeway—although still

The Park Board commissioners in 1919 were (left to right) W.S. Rawlings, Robert Eldon, G.W. Hutchings, Jonathan Rogers, M.S. Logan, A.C.J. Weeks, and A.S. Wootton.

The City of Vancouver's welcome sign on Highway 99.

unfinished—had a great impact on the park. On one Sunday in July 1919, *five hundred cars* tried to pass through the Brockton Point area *every eight minutes*, the first traffic jam ever recorded in Stanley Park.[4]

The Park Board commissioners had their work cut out for them to handle the success of the largest of the twenty parks now within their jurisdiction.

Though the causeway plan had been approved in 1916 and work began right away, progress was slow. It was 1926—ten years—before the causeway was completed. By then, little thought was given to these early Douglas-fir comrades—the primitive crossing and the big fir—two of the many legacy trees of Stanley Park.

Perhaps coincidentally, the WELCOME TO VANCOUVER sign that now greets drivers heading south on Highway 99 marks where they once stood.

8

Growing Together

The woods are made for the hunters of dreams,
The brooks for the fishers of song;
To the hunters who hunt for the gunless game
The streams and the wood belong

"The Bloodless Sportsman," Sam Walter Foss (1858–1911)

Similarities and Differences

I AM INTRIGUED by how similar we humans are to trees. Adult beings, whether trees or humans, protect their offspring until they are sufficiently mature to withstand what life throws—or blows—at them.

These days, we have incredible technology that allows scientists to understand more about trees than ever before. These dendrologists (tree scientists) have determined that the trunk and branches of trees employ a very slow pulse of contraction and expansion to send water up and out to every branchlet and leaf. This pulse has even been given the term *heartbeat*.[1]

In another way that humans anthropomorphize trees, it is now being claimed that trees breathe in during the day (the time when they are actually releasing more oxygen) and they breathe out at night (the time when they release carbon dioxide). One slow breath for every twenty-four hours. The old wives' tale recommending the removal at night of all plants from the room of someone who is ill is based on this ancient awareness of plants' release of carbon dioxide at night. The breathing-in-and-breathing-out claim leans on evidence

in time-lapse photography that shows trees lowering their branches at night.[2]

This idea is extended to the suggestion that the northern hemisphere of Earth breathes in every summer and breathes out every winter. One slow planetary breath for every twelve months.

Whereas plants grow where they are planted ("the apple doesn't grow far from the tree"), we humans sometimes uproot ourselves and venture farther afield than our parents would ever dare.

Some trees live for centuries and even millennia in ideal conditions. They withstand change, stabilize and slow dehydration of the soil, and moderate the atmosphere. They move moisture inland and withstand extreme temperatures and weather conditions.

Humans, on the other hand, live an average of only eighty years, dig up the soil, speed up soil dehydration, heat the atmosphere, and cut down trees. We increase the presence of carbon dioxide in the atmosphere, we waste water, and our creations (buildings, vehicles, and travel routes) are susceptible to extreme weather conditions. We seek distraction, entertainment, fame, and wealth.

Don't get me wrong. I'm not against humans. After all, I'm one of us. I just think we can learn a lot from trees, from their equanimity, humility, stability, solidity, and generosity.

Crown Shyness

If you are lucky enough to stand inside a grove of mature trees, look up and you'll observe something called *crown shyness*. Their crowns don't appear to touch; they may interlace, but they don't mingle. This appears to happen only with deciduous trees.

There are two theories for what is going on. One is that trees of the same species avoid both being shaded by and shading each other. They take up space that is not already filled, allowing each other space to grow and breathe and capture the sun's rays. The opposing theory is that stormy weather breaks off branches that are very close to each other. I suspect a mixture of both theories is at work.

How does this work with humans? Sometimes we hold the space for someone near and dear to grow up beside us, to shine in our light. We nurture each other, in a feminine, yin way. Other times, we compete with others relentlessly for the alpha position, using our yang energy.

Living and Dying

Trees and animals differ in how they live and die. I'm not talking about the obvious way animals (us humans included) are able to move from place to place, and make sounds, and choose our food and our mates and our path in life. I'm referring to the fact that an animal is continuously regenerating the cells of its body until it dies, physically, as a

TOP Three dogwoods that have been planted near the Vancouver Aquarium support each other as they grow together.

BOTTOM This western redcedar buckled under the weight of its own bulk before it died.

A tree that fell in the forest is providing nourishment to the flora around it.

whole. A tree, on the other hand, does not regenerate its individual cells.

Each year the cambium—the living and dividing layer of cells that creates the phloem of the bark and the xylem of the heartwood—grows new cells externally and allows the old internal cells to die. This is how trees grow greater in girth and height. This is how the bark continues to push out, cracking and furrowing and grooving and bulging.

The heartwood of a tree—the wood that humans value so highly—is dead, formed over the years. A new living ring of cells enwraps the heartwood each year. In a cut log, we can see that the ring is made up of darker and lighter parts. It is darker in spring, when the year's growth begins (numerous new cells are packed closely together) and becomes paler through the heat of summer and during the slower growth of fall. This makes the annual rings easy to count.

Trees and animals also differ in how they die.

Even though we humans have difficulty pinpointing the *moment* of a person's death, we can almost always point to the *day* of death. The death of an animal is lightning-speed faster than that of a tree. The death of a tree is a very drawn-out affair, taking years and even decades, as the tree changes from being healthy to having its health impinged on in some way, to losing more of its branches than would occur normally through self-pruning, to becoming a standing snag, and finally to falling to the forest floor. The decomposition—the composting—of one tree provides the soil for the birth and regeneration of many others.

When a tree falls in the forest, its fallen form—minerals, fibre, and glucose—nourishes all the other life forms in its environment. The forest floor becomes littered with coarse woody debris, such as the branches of trees that drop their lower branches as they grow taller, leaves and needles, cones and winged seeds, and flaking bark. These coarse woody remains are essential in the ecology of healthy old-growth forest. Because of the wet climate here on the West Coast (Vancouver receives over 1,150 millimetres—over 45 inches—of rain annually), moss grows over this coarse woody debris, giving Stanley Park's forest the appearance of being blanketed with a vibrant green.

When a tree snaps in a windstorm, it's called a *windsnap*. When a tree with shallow roots falls over, the roots tear out of the earth in a clump, bringing rocks and small plants with them; the tree is called a *windthrow* or *blowdown*, and its roots are called a *root wad*. The upended root wad with its soil becomes home for other creatures. I've learned that few trees have deep taproots, and that the depth of the root depends on the soil conditions rather than on the tree species.

I have two favourite root wads on Tatlow Trail. One is incredibly wide, spanning a bend in the path. Around the other, rain has washed the embedded earth away to reveal a pattern that is more intricate than a tapestry (see image on page 75).

Fallen trees become nurse logs for seedling trees, especially for western hemlocks.

Walking through Stanley Park's trails, we can see trees in every stage of birth, midlife, dying, and death. Some examples are visible in open areas.

On the eastern edge of the Shakespeare and Perennial Garden is a western redcedar that has half a dozen stories to tell. If you sit on one of the benches that surround its 15-metre girth, you will hear its stories. It was logged, perhaps several times. Or maybe the logging was unsuccessful the first time. The squarish holes at different heights tell us where the springboards were perched at different levels in the 1860s or 1870s. But what is amazing is how the tree stump—after being completely logged—has regrown itself with three new trunks. And maybe one of those is a different species: a seed from a nearby hemlock

A western redcedar with half a dozen stories to tell.

fell and found fertile soil. This western redcedar tells a story of survival.

We have a great deal in common with trees: living, producing offspring, dying. But we live out our years quite differently from our leafy neighbours. Trees have much to teach us if only we are open to learn.

9

The Hollow Tree

Give me again my hollow tree,
A crust of bread, and liberty.

Imitations of Horace, Alexander Pope (1688–1744)

BEING AT THE ocean or beside a lake is good for us. We feel good. We
have entered the realm of negative ions—the ions that make us feel good
because they neutralize all the free radicals that result from our natural
body processes or that exist as environmental toxins. Therefore, we like
spending time by the ocean. The forest is also an atmosphere of negative
ions, so it's good for us for all the same reasons. Being in Stanley Park is
an ocean-*and*-forest experience. No wonder it attracts so many people
each day.

Plants and animals create the greatest symbiosis possible, because
while both plants and animals respire (use oxygen to release energy from
sugars), plants also release excess oxygen from photosynthesis, and that
oxygen is essential for animal life. What a brilliant balance. Now, if we
could *really* balance how we live together . . .

When settlers first encountered the massive trees in Stanley Park,
they measured around their trunks and described them by their circumference: "spruce tree 44 feet in circumference."

Do you see the man in the photo on the next page? He looks tiny. And
just look at the ferns and moss growing on that tree's trunk and branches!

"Cedar tree 38 feet in circumference . . . 46 feet . . . 50 feet . . . 60 feet
. . . 80 feet in circumference." One tree was variously described as either

RIGHT Spruce tree that is 44 feet in circumference. Notice the man in a frock coat standing to the left of massive tree.

▶ OPPOSITE, CLOCKWISE FROM TOP LEFT
Cheerie Auto Park Tally-Ho in Stanley Park in 1908.

The photograph taken by the Bailey Bros. photographer who is pictured taking that photo in the bottom photo.

Staged photograph taken at Prospect Point, Stanley Park, by R.H. Trueman and Co. in 1891.

60 feet (18 metres) or 80 feet (24 metres) in circumference, depending on where they measured it—measuring standards were not yet in place. After a while, it became easier to refer to it as the Hollow Tree.

"Harold, let's go to the park this afternoon to see that cedar tree they say is sixty feet in circumference."

"Do you mean the Hollow Tree, Myrtle? That's a wonderful idea."

"Let's go by tally-ho!"

"Ah, yes."

In the early days, people visited Stanley Park to play sports, ride around Park Drive, admire the wonderful views, and gaze in awe at the massive trees. They travelled in phaetons (light, horse-drawn carriages),

more open horse-drawn carriages, and tally-hos, as well as on horseback (hence Bridle Path) and bicycles, and on foot, and later in cars. Not very different from today, except today people drive in cars, travel in buses, cycle, rollerblade, jog, and walk, with or without dogs, but nobody travels on horseback. Oh, except for the Vancouver Police Mounted Squad; what better way to get around the park!

Professional photographers took to the streets—and the forests—in those days, providing us today with a fabulous visual heritage, even if the images were sometimes staged.

Do you see the photographer standing on a stump in the very centre of the bottom photo on the opposite page? How tall and

BIG TREE, STANLEY PARK
Sam Brighouse, mounted,
beard, 1890, Bailey photo

TOP Early settler Sam Brighouse (sporting a beard, mounted) with other Vancouver pioneers at the Hollow Tree in 1890. Brighouse was a Park Board commissioner in 1888 and 1889.

BOTTOM Group portrait showing Mr. and Mrs. J.F. Grimmett and others in front of the Hollow Tree sometime between 1905 and 1907.

broad might that tree have been, before it was felled and became a popular stump to take pictures from? The location was then called the Lookout, later Prospect Point Lookout. The photographer is one of the Bailey brothers, either Charles or William. The top right photo on page 67 is the picture he took that day. See if you can recognize the same people milling about the gazebo by the clothes they were wearing.

Charles Bailey, professional photographer, also waited at the Hollow Tree. That tree was Vancouver's biggest tourist attraction in more ways than one. On the way home from their tally-ho outing to the park, visitors would stop at the seven- or eight-hundred-year-old western redcedar, position themselves, and hold it, hold it . . . Done! The moment would be captured on celluloid for future generations.

Decade after decade, people had their photographs taken inside the already long-dead tree, its trunk surrounding an area 5 by 7 metres (16 by 23 feet)—big enough to house a vehicle. They would back up their horses, buggies, Cadillacs, and bicycles, clamber all over it, and arrange themselves importantly inside and around the most revered relic in the park. Occasionally, there have been even bigger visitors, such as the trained elephant who brought his trainers and swept a woman off her feet.[1]

Reading in 2018 about this hollow red-cedar, I find it fascinating that media articles age the tree variously from seven hundred years old (CBC in 2017) to a thousand years old (*Vancouver Observer* in 2011). Since it has no tree rings, being hollow, determining age is very difficult.

In 1965, the Hollow Tree needed to be braced with iron to remain standing. This was a few years after Typhoon Freda in 1962. Then, in December 2006, in a relentless windstorm that reached hurricane strength, the Hollow Tree was damaged, seemingly beyond repair, and left leaning at a perilous angle. The Park Board voted to let this piece of woody heritage go to its final resting place. However, Vancouver citizens and corporations were having none of that! The tree had been revered as an emblem of the city's history, listed on the Vancouver Heritage Register and the Vancouver Heritage Tree Inventory, and recognized by Parks Canada as a Level One Cultural Resource.[2]

Heritage consultants and conservationists, engineers, arborists, and big-tree specialists came together to form the Stanley Park Hollow Tree Conservation Society. Over a

two-year period, the volunteer members provided the Park Board with a thirty-page conservation plan,[3] raised funds, and stabilized and restored this piece of the park. Now, surrounded by information boards describing its history, the Hollow Tree will stand tall for many more decades.

Something that will last just as long but will be seen in a wholly different light is Douglas Coupland's gold-coloured precise replica of the Hollow Tree, *Golden Tree*. He created it for the public space in front of a real estate developer's corporate presence in Marpole, near the SkyTrain station on Cambie. Below is the description from the website of this visual artist,

Wife, sister, sister-in-law, and children of Edgar G. Baynes, Vancouver Park Board commissioner from 1924 to 1938. Photograph taken in 1908 at the Hollow Tree.
COURTESY OF
E.G. BAYNES'S GRANDSON
DAVID WOOLLIAMS.

novelist, non-fiction author, playwright, and Generation X thinker. (Forgive the fact that the write-up makes Coupland seem rather tall; the writer intended to describe his sculpture!)

> Standing 43 feet tall, Coupland has set the sculpture in front of a 25-foot by 40-foot image of Stanley Park, which has been installed above the front entrance to Intracorp's MC2 development at Cambie Street and SE Marine Drive. Made out of steel-reinforced resin and fiberglass and encased in a gold finish, the piece took more than 6,000 hours to fabricate.[4]

Have you had your photograph taken in front of Stanley Park's Hollow Tree?

10

Trail Trees

Old-growth forests, such as those found within Stanley Park,
have long and dynamic histories to share . . .

The term "old-growth" often generates confusion. I use it to describe
a structural stage of forest stand dynamics, defined by the presence of
several structural attributes, such as relatively large trees, large standing
dead trees, large logs on the ground, and an open, stratified canopy . . .

None of Stanley Park is pristine, but much is old-growth,
and some contains trees >600 years old.

Vancouver Big Tree Hiking Guide website, Ira Sutherland, forest ecologist

BEING A WOMAN in my senior years, I don't want to hike the trails alone. I know I would probably be safe, but I probably wouldn't be too relaxed. And my husband would rather hike in the city than in the park; he thinks there's more to see there. I wondered how I was going to get to know the trail trees.

So I began by reading about them.

Today, big-tree specialists measure a tree by its height, girth, and crown spread, using the tangent method for height, the distance around the trunk at 1.3 to 1.5 metres (4 feet 3 inches to 5 feet) above the ground for circumference, and various very technical methods for establishing crown spread. Tree specialists also discern whether a tree is single- or multi-trunked. And whether what appears to be one trunk is actually from the merging of a number of tree trunks as they grew broader in girth. Measuring trees involves an elaborate, very

technical scientific process. Several websites focus on the tallest, the biggest, and the oldest trees, and the methods of measuring them.[1]

As I've said, I am not a tree specialist, I'm a tree enthusiast. What I know is that when I see a really big tree, whether it's a massive bigleaf maple or a towering Douglas-fir, I say, "Look at *you*!" I am in awe of their abundance, their solidity, their uniqueness.

It's the same when I see an abundance of redcedar cones or maple samaras (the winged seeds that move like helicopters) or a showering of catkins. I am equally full of admiration for the small hemlock saplings that grow on windthrows and for the ferns that nestle into the crooks of tree branches and among seedlings.

The massive trees in Stanley Park, a temperate rainforest, have always held fascination for Vancouverites. The photograph on the opposite page was taken in 1901. What I find fascinating about it is not only the perspective provided by the woman in her modest Victorian outfit among the "forest giants" but also the relationship between the woman and the photographer. She appears in multiple early photographs from archival collections. Was she a photographer's model? A photographer's wife? Were all the photographs taken on the same day?

Female visitor to Stanley Park is dwarfed by the massive
rainforest trees.

A DRIVEWAY THROUGH THE FOREST GIANTS, STANLEY PARK.

ABOVE Park Drive winds through the forest giants in 1917.

RIGHT A man rests at the foot of a western redcedar.

Another photograph, taken in 1917 of Stanley Park Drive, shows more forest giants, Douglas-firs and western redcedars. Notice the two small figures on the right of the picture; again, they provide perspective.

On the left is an 1891 photo of a man resting against a massive tree, a western redcedar. He looks very settled. Note the way the bark has buckled from the weight of the tree above.

I persuaded my husband to walk a few trails with me. Tatlow Walk became one of our favourites. You can reach it from the walk around Lost Lagoon, by taking the path that branches north and crossing North Lagoon Drive at the crosswalk.

If you walk the trails in Stanley Park, you will find your favourite trails, tall trees, root

wads, tree trunks. Some monument trees are alive and some are in their half-life, giving life to the organisms around them.

For instance, the tree known as the *National Geographic* tree will be in its half-life for many years to come, having fallen during the windstorm of 2006. When *National Geographic* photographed it in the 1970s, this western redcedar was the oldest standing tree in the park, with an estimated age of a thousand years.[2] Its decomposing remains are now barely visible along the Third Beach Trail, having been overgrown with forest understorey (see page 77).

Several of the tallest Douglas-firs in the park contain eagles' nests, which is not really surprising, because eagles, even when they're mating and raising eaglets, want to command the best view possible. There's one such tree directly east of the Theatre Under the Stars ticket offices; you have to walk through the Rock Garden and behind the Harding memorial to find it.

A group of eagle-nest trees is visible east of Pipeline Road. Several have lost their tops and several are standing deadheads. (What terms I've learned!) They are growing to the east of Tunnel Trail (off Pipeline Road north of Beaver Lake). Just don't get too close. You don't want nest debris falling on top of you! Eagles are messy nest-builders and eaters.

Take another look at the 1911 map in the introduction and see where the 10s are—they denote the location of remarkable trail trees. It's also interesting to see on this old map where the record-breaking trees were

FROM LEFT TO RIGHT
On the trail.

A root wad on Tatlow Trail.

The tangle of roots on the underside of the root wad on Tatlow Trail create a beautiful tapestry.

in the past. Since those days, the park has suffered three major windstorms: the Great Storm in 1934, Typhoon Freda in 1962, and the hurricane-force windstorm of 2006.

That 2006 windstorm created absolute havoc in the park. It cleared some areas irrevocably—one such area became the expanded miniature-railway route. Others just allowed space for young trees to grow tall. People in Vancouver donated millions for forest restoration and public safety.

When I drove Stanley Park Drive after the storm to see what had happened, I wondered whether the park could *ever* recover from such devastation. The losses were heartbreaking. Ten thousand trees ... gone.

But it has recovered, in its own way.

Another favourite trail tree of mine is the two-spirit carving on a stump. To get there, take Bridle Path from Second Beach and turn left (northwest) on Rawlings Trail. Soon, an opening on your right will invite you in. Carved sometime in the 1990s, this sculpture displays an Indigenous energy. The 2 in LGBTQ2 refers to *two-spirit*, a term used by Indigenous North Americans to refer to their conception of gender variance. While one of the faces carved into this stump is clearly visible, the second is wearing away with time and weather.[3]

I hear that other trail trees offer places for sacred ritual, Indigenous harvest,[4] meditation, and beauty worthy of a work of art.

◄ OPPOSITE A two-spirit carving on a stump.

TOP Undergrowth hides what's left of the fallen *National Geographic* tree.

BOTTOM These plaques at Prospect Point list the many donations that poured in to restore Stanley Park after the windstorm of 2006 that damaged over ten thousand trees.

11

Siwash Rock

Unique, and so distinct from its surroundings as to suggest rather the handicraft of man than a whim of Nature, it looms up at the entrance to the Narrows, a symmetrical column of solid grey stone. There are no similar formations within the range of vision, or indeed within many a day's paddle up and down the coast. Amongst all the wonders, the natural beauties that encircle Vancouver, the marvels of mountains, shaped into crouching lions and brooding beavers, the yawning canyons, the stupendous forest firs and cedars, Siwash Rock stands as distinct, as individual, as if dropped from another sphere.

"The Siwash Rock," *Legends of Vancouver*, E. Pauline Johnson, 1911

EVER SINCE THE earliest photographs were taken of Siwash Rock, a tree has been growing on top of this stone column. The photograph on the next page, taken less than two decades after Stanley Park was named, shows a tree on top and a healthy shrub on the opposite side, with seven men below.

Pauline Johnson—who also liked to be known by her Mohawk name, Tekahionwake—tells the story of Siwash Rock in *Legends of Vancouver*. It's her interpretation of a Squamish legend told to her by Squamish leader Chief Joe Capilano. She mentions two other rocks, known as Siwash Rock's wife and baby. These are to be found "if you penetrate the hollows in the woods near Siwash Rock."

And yet it seems the labels of these rocks shifted, for in an 1890s photo, a woman sits atop "Siwash Rock's wife," smiling and sketching; Siwash Rock is in the background and no woods are in evidence.[1]

◀ OPPOSITE

A Douglas-fir grows on top of Siwash Rock.

79

Seven men have climbed over the rocks to stand in the shadow of Siwash Rock.

Major Matthews recorded other Squamish legends attached to Siwash Rock in *Early Vancouver*. Yet another smaller rock known as Sunz was held to be Siwash Rock's first wife.[2] This rock, which also once grew a tree on top, is located at the original Prospect Point lighthouse and boathouse (latitude 49.314 N | longitude 123.141 W). As is often the case with mythology, there are multiple-story perspectives that explain the presence of the rocks.

Johnson's romanticized retelling of the Siwash Rock legend relays how a young chief and his pregnant wife swam in the waters of the narrows to prove their purity on the day she was to give birth. They believed this would give their child the best chance for a successful life.

> Presently he took her ashore, and smilingly she crept away under the giant trees. "I must be alone," she said, "but come to me at sunrise: you will not find me alone then."[3]

The young man kept swimming, determined to keep his vigil until he knew the moment of his child's birth had come.

Four giants in an enormous canoe—divine agents of "the Sagalie Tyee"—came paddling through the strait. They commanded the young chief to get out of their way. He refused, explaining his dedication to his task of epitomizing clean fatherhood. At that moment, "there floated from out the forest a faint, strange, compelling sound."

The tallest of the divine beings stood in the canoe to pronounce:

"You have defied what interferes with your child's chance for a clean life … You have placed that child's future before all things, and for this the Sagalie Tyee commands us to make you forever a pattern for your tribe. You shall never die, but you shall stand through all the thousands of years to come, where all eyes can see you. You shall live, live, live as an indestructible monument to Clean Fatherhood."

The four men lifted their paddles and the handsome young chief swam inshore; as his feet touched the line where sea and land met he was transformed into stone.

Then the four men said, "His wife and child must ever be near him; they shall not die, but live also." And they, too, were turned into stone.[4]

Pauline Johnson was only in her late forties when she moved to Vancouver, yet she was already ill. She died in 1913, a few days before her fifty-second birthday. Her funeral was the largest Vancouver had seen. Her ashes were scattered not far from Siwash Rock, at Ferguson Point, and in 1922 a cairn was erected at the site.

Siwash Rock.

When a tree growing on Siwash Rock died, the Vancouver Park Board decided to plant another one in its place. The first one they planted didn't catch. But the next one, a Douglas-fir, did. Looking at this monolith while walking the seawall counter-clockwise, I think the tree either has three trunks or is in fact three trees, and one of them might be deciduous.

In 2017, the Park Board began discussions with First Nations about changing Siwash Rock's name to something close to *Slahkayulsh*, Salish for "standing man."

I clambered over some slippery rocks on the beach to take the shot on the previous page. I am pleased that it makes the rock look very much like a man with a topknot, quite a popular look these days.

12

One of the Seven Sisters

There is a well-known trail in Stanley Park that leads to what I always
love to call the "Cathedral Trees"—that group of some half-dozen forest
giants that arch overhead with such superb loftiness.

"The Lure in Stanley Park," *Legends of Vancouver*, E. Pauline Johnson, 1911

IN HER LAST book (published by her friends in 1911), *The Legends of Vancouver*, Pauline Johnson writes about the grove of western red-cedars and Douglas-firs that became known as the Seven Sisters. In flowery language styled after her favourite authors such as Byron, Tennyson, Keats, Browning, and Milton, Johnson compares the holy majesty of these giants with the holy design of a man-made cathedral.

> But in all the world there is no cathedral whose marble or onyx columns can vie with those straight, clean, brown tree-boles that teem with the sap and blood of life. There is no fresco that can rival the delicacy of lace-work they have festooned between you and the far skies. No tiles, no mosaic or inlaid marbles are as fascinating as the bare, russet, fragrant floor outspreading about their feet. They are the acme of Nature's architecture, and in building them she has out-rivalled all her erstwhile conceptions. She will never originate a more faultless design, never erect a more perfect edifice. But the divinely moulded trees and the man-made cathedral have one exquisite characteristic in common. It is the atmosphere of holiness.[1]

An Edwardian woman visits the Seven Sisters in 1905.

Like the Edwardian woman who visited the Seven Sisters in 1905 (see photo), I have stood among these revered giants—what's left of them—and wondered about the past that these woody sentinels experienced. I've thought of all those who have visited this place, people such as Johnson and Emily Carr.

I walked there on Earth Day, April 22, 2018. What better day could there be for a walk in the park, photographing light and shadow, leaf and bole? I could hear planes flying overhead, freeway traffic going by not far away, and a bird whistling sweetly and incessantly.

I sat on a very cold rock in what was once the Seven Sisters grove of trees.

They became so popular for visiting, photographing, and painting that a special trail was cut to reach them—Cathedral Trail—and a welcoming arch was erected nearby on Tatlow Walk; you can see it in a 1928 photograph taken by James Crookall.

Their fame during Stanley Park's first sixty-five years proved to be their undoing. In the early 1950s, the Park Board decided the tall trees were so elderly they were no longer safe and, for park goers' safety, should be removed.

Now the simple statement under Plexiglas resting in front of this locale suggests there are now "seven large stumps" instead of Seven Sisters.

Looking around on Earth Day, I saw some very broad stumps no more than a metre high. Big trees have grown up out of some of these stumps. Tall trees big enough to dwarf a person grow along each of the nearby trails—Cathedral Trail, Bridle Path, Lees Trail, and Tatlow Walk. All around, enormous Douglas-firs and western redcedars and slimmer western hemlocks reach for the sky, straining for more sunlight, their source of energy.

Given that there are many very tall and aged-looking trees all around the Seven Sisters location, I think that the original name of *Seven* Sisters was a bit vague. Pauline Johnson counted "some half dozen." I count four big stumps and two smaller ones.

That makes me wonder: Were there six or seven here originally? Or more? Was the name for these trees borrowed from the seven elms circling a walnut tree in Greater London—in an area now called Seven Sisters? London was the native home of many immigrants to Western Canada.

Counting these stumps and trying to identify which were the original seven, I compare the photograph I took with the ones from 1905, 1928, and the plaque on the ground. I recognize the leftmost tree from the photograph.

It's still standing?

That western redcedar with the large burl—the most northerly tree of the group—looks very much like the tree that's on the extreme left of the commemorative photograph in front of these remaining

contenders for the Seven Sisters title. Yes, it is! This is one of the original seven! (If there were seven.)

I recognize the burl partway up the trunk, the right-angled branch that's preparing to be one branch of a candelabra (*candelabra* is real forestry terminology!), and the way the trunk blends into the earth. I am thrilled with this discovery.

As a centennial gift to the park on September 27, 1988, the Park Board planted seven young Douglas-fir trees on Bridle Path to replace the original Seven Sisters. The replantation trees are hard for me—a non-arborist—to distinguish from the tall trees around them. Once these young trees become strong enough to take over from their neighbouring giants, they will shoot up in height. Then they might start to rival the original seven.

Meanwhile, I will return to feel the history embedded in this single sibling.

◄ OPPOSITE A few of the Seven Sisters plus an archway in 1928 in a photograph taken by James Crookall.

ABOVE One of the original Seven Sisters.

PART II

The First Trees Are Planted

13

Martha Smith's Lilac Bushes

In one place in the verge of the Wood I saw an old Canoe suspended five or six feet from the ground between two Trees & containing some decayed human bones wrapped up in Mats & carefully coverd [sic] over with Boards; . . . it would appear that this is the general mode of entombing their dead in this Country . . . to place them out of the reach of Bears, Wolves & other Animals & prevent them from digging up or offering any violence to recent bodies after interment.

Archibald Menzies's journal entry of June 12, 1792, while anchored at Birch Bay, Washington. From *Menzies' Journal of Vancouver's Voyage.*

WHEN STANLEY PARK first became a public park, a number of Squamish, Musqueam, and Tsleil-Waututh families lived at Brockton Point, Whoi Whoi, Chaythoos, and Deadman's Island, all flat areas near the shore. Immigrants to Canada also moved in to make the peninsula their home, marrying Indigenous women, building simple homes, and surrounding them with gardens.

As Jean Barman, professor emeritus of Cultural Studies, History of Education, and Indigenous Studies at the University of British Columbia, points out, these families fell between the cracks—between the reserve and the new city of Vancouver. A Fellow of the Royal Society of Canada, Barman describes the way of life and the challenges for those living in the park in *Stanley Park's Secret: The Forgotten Families of Whoi Whoi, Kanaka Ranch and Brockton Point.*[1]

One such family was Martha and Peter Smith's. Martha Thompson was of mixed heritage—her mother was from a First Nation in the

◄ OPPOSITE Martha Smith's lilac bushes bloom in May.

Martha Smith's lilac bushes grow between the pedestrian and cycle paths.

Fraser Valley, and her father was unidentified. Peter Smith was the namesake of his father, a man born on the Azores Islands, an archipelago off Portugal in the mid-Atlantic. His mother was Indigenous. Peter worked on the docks as a longshoreman.

Martha and Peter had met while attending Coqualeetza Home, a residential school run by the Women's Missionary Society and the Board of Home Missions of the Methodist Church. The school was in the Fraser Valley, on the shores of Luckakuck Creek in Sardis, BC. In later years, the Smiths sent four of their seven children to the school at Coqualeetza.

After marrying in the late 1890s, the couple settled at Brockton Point, where Peter had grown up. Martha planted a couple of lilac trees, perhaps around 1896, to show the people at Coqualeetza how settled she was. In 1904, Peter and Martha sought title to their Brockton Point property. Called "squatters" by the city's lawyer, the couple was living on shaky ground.

Beginning in 1923, the City of Vancouver and the Government of Canada held trials to dispossess all those living in the park of their domiciles. A public park was not deemed a place where people could live, unless those people could prove to the satisfaction of white law that they had been living in their residences continuously for sixty years, that is, from April 21, 1863, twenty-three years before Vancouver was incorporated. Martha and Peter Smith and their neighbours could not.

Eventually, in May 1925, the Supreme Court of Canada decided that these interracial families had no right to remain in the park. Yet the Vancouver Park Board was slow to move them out. Martha, widowed during "the eviction trials," signed an agreement to become a tenant of the city within the park for the rent of a dollar a month. This lasted until 1931, when a house in East Vancouver was made available to her. Instead, she chose to move to Washington state, where she remarried.

Unlike the oak that was ceremonially planted in Brockton Point a few years later (see the next chapter), Martha Smith's lilac bushes are seen and enjoyed by thousands of park goers every year, even if those visitors do not realize the piece of park history to which the lilacs bear witness.

Her lilacs continue to grow well on Brockton Point, between the Harry Winston Jerome statue in the west and the Nine O'Clock Gun in the east, between the bicycle path and the seawall.

14

An Oak at Brockton Oval

A stone's throw away, near the main entrance of the Brockton Point Grounds . . . a little group of prominent men who love the oak were gathered around a specimen of the emblem of Old England, which was being planted to mark the coronation of the King. The joy of the event was stayed by reverence, and in days to come it is to be hoped that the little stranger . . . will thrive and grow to cast a grateful shade on children, and refresh the memories of the week now past.

"Planting of the King's Oak," *The Vancouver Daily Province*, August 11, 1902

EARLY ON, ONE way or another, Brockton Point was associated with things that went awry. But about the time King Edward VII's coronation oak was planted, things had finally settled down. Let me describe the events that led up to that planting.

First, the point was named for Francis Brockton, an engineer aboard HMS *Plumper*, a Royal Navy sloop surveying British Columbia's coastline. In the course of surveying, Brockton identified a vein of coal, a promise of riches that was never fulfilled. To honour Brockton's discovery, Governor James Douglas (later knighted by Queen Victoria for his service to the empire) gave the name Brockton Point to the most easterly promontory of the government reserve near the frontier settlement of Gastown. This happened around 1859.

The unfulfilled promise of coal is also reflected in the name for the entire harbour—Coal Harbour.

Then came Captain Edward Stamp's unsuccessful attempt to establish a logging and milling operation at Brockton Point.

That ended with the company's move to Hastings Mill.

We jump ahead nineteen years, to November 1886, when three men climbed into a small boat and rowed over to the Government Reserve—not yet called Stanley Park—in search of a flat place suitable for playing a game of cricket. They were Alderman L.A. Hamilton, the chief surveyor for the Canadian Pacific Railway (CPR); Major Gardner Johnson, an ardent cricketer; and A.E. Beck, an athlete and law student who later became the first registrar of BC's Supreme Court. Beck later recalled,

> We reached Brockton Point, clambered over the boulder-strewn shore, and plunged into the forest, which stood in its original state save for such large trees as loggers had removed; there were no roads or trails.
>
> We broke through to the far side, to the Narrows. Mr. Hamilton pointed out the beauty of the site, encompassed by the sea, the snow-capped mountains; and, it was level.[1]

Beck suggested that the young men working in offices and stores in Vancouver would not have the time and money to spare to row over for a game. "I remarked that it was a truly beautiful place, but would take a 'million dollars' to clear it."[2]

A slightly better, though not ideal, cricket field was chosen—a sloping patch of Cambie Street held by the CPR, which had recently built the final leg of its transcontinental rail line linking Vancouver with Ontario.

In January 1889, four months after the naming of Stanley Park, Dr. Bell-Irving of the Rifle Association requested that the open area at Brockton Point be made into a shooting range. The park commissioners turned down the request, believing it would be "dangerous to pedestrians and others."[3]

The same year, the Vancouver Cricket Club was formed, and its members completed what Captain Stamp had begun and cleared the field at Brockton. Cricket games began.

In 1892, the City of Vancouver (not the Park Board) built a long, covered grandstand that could seat about fifteen hundred sports spectators, on a level area west of the cricket field. Brockton Oval became popular for women's field hockey and men's rugby.

People came by ferry to watch lacrosse and field hockey games, bicycle races, and athletic events at Brockton Field. The ferry landed them near Martha Smith's lilac bushes, close to the location of what is now called the Nine O'Clock Gun (though when that "12-pounder muzzle-loaded naval cannon" was installed in 1898, it was not known as such).[4]

The fact that the City of Vancouver maintained control of Brockton Point—an area within Stanley Park—became a sore point with the Vancouver Park Board. Thus began an ongoing struggle that would not be resolved until the spring of 1913, when the city relinquished its control.

After all these unsuccessful flurries, we have finally reached a more settled time—and the planting of a commemorative tree. The Brockton Point Association decided to plant an English oak to commemorate the coronation of Edward VII and Alexandra of Denmark as king and queen of the United Kingdom and the British Dominions. The president of the Brockton Point Association, was given the honour of planting the tree.

This took place on August 9, 1902, a day when the Caledonian Games were being played at Brockton Oval. The association members chose a site near both the Brockton Pavilion and the eastern main entrance to the Oval's grounds. Mr. Campbell Sweeney, their president, personally planted the "fine young oak."[5]

Apparently, a plaque was set in the ground below the tree, but it is no longer there. This English oak is the first tree planted commemoratively in Stanley Park, and yet there is nothing on the ground now to mark its history.

Soon after the planting of that first oak, park gardeners planted a long row of English oaks nearby. Nowadays, these fine oaks create a north–south *allée* with a low evergreen hedge, dividing flat Brockton

The King Edward VII oak tree in 1924. It had already grown quite large.

LEFT An *allée* of English oaks and a western redcedar hedge separate Brockton Oval from Brockton Field.

RIGHT The current grandstand at Brockton Oval in between concerts.

▶ OPPOSITE The English oak planted to commemorate the coronation of King Edward VII. Photo taken in 2018.

Oval and the current grandstand in the west from sloping Brockton Field in the east. The hedge replaces the original stave fence. The oaks are fine specimens. English oaks are also sometimes called pedunculate oaks because of their long peduncles (stalks) that hold the flowers, and later the acorns, to the stems. (In contrast, the acorns on native Garry oaks, *Quercus garryana*, are sessile, meaning they have no peduncles. Also, English oak leaves are nearly sessile— they have no petioles, or leaf stalks—while Garry oak leaves have 2-centimetre-long petioles.)

A quarter of a century after the planting of that tree, in 1927, the Brockton Clubhouse was built strategically between the field and the Oval, to support both. It was built near the King Edward VII oak tree.

In the twenty-first century, Brockton Pavilion is a private facility within the park known as the Cricket & Rugby Pavilion at Brockton Oval.[6] It is home to the Evergreens Rugby Club, the BC Mainland Cricket League, and the Vancouver Rugby Union.

In the years since the oak was planted, a large maple tree growing close to the Brockton Clubhouse has been misidentified

The English oak planted to commemorate the coronation of King Edward VII. Photo taken in 2018.

in photographs and on websites as the King Edward VII oak.

Regardless, the English oak has grown taller and fuller than the native maple, and cannot be mistaken for anything else, especially when it is in leaf. Stand under its generous shade and admire its spread.

15

Around the Oppenheimer Bust

In the fall of 1909, a committee was formed to build a memorial to David Oppenheimer, former Mayor of Vancouver. Oppenheimer was an entrepreneur from Germany and served four 1-year terms as Mayor. He donated land for city parks and for the Rogers sugar refinery. The memorial committee planned to hire Augustus St. Gaudens to build a memorial gate to connect Stanley Park to the City in honour of Oppenheimer, but they found out St. Gaudens was dead.

"David Oppenheimer," Public Art Registry, City of Vancouver website

MAYORS AND PARK superintendents come and go. Some have been remembered by park trails named for them. Vancouver's second mayor, David Oppenheimer, is remembered with a bronze bust (latitude 49.2904 N | longitude 123.146 W) that welcomes visitors and Vancouverites to the park at the Beach Avenue entrance.[1]

Oppenheimer had travelled to North America from his home in Blieskastel, Germany, when that area was still known as Bavaria. He knew what beautiful parks were all about. For the four years that he was Vancouver's second mayor, from 1888 to 1891, Oppenheimer worked without pay. Funding was short; Vancouver was still recovering financially from the devastating fire that had burned the young city to ashes on June 13, 1886. Fortunately, David and his brother Isaac, two of the five Oppenheimer siblings who left Germany for North America together, had based their southern BC business on groceries. A growing city needs to feed its hungry men, women, and children.

Monument to Mayor
David Oppenheimer, 1911.

Oppenheimer was the mayor in office when Ottawa gave permission for the military reserve on the peninsula to become a public park. He opened Stanley Park—the first one to pronounce the park's name publicly—on September 27, 1888, on the far side of the park, in an area called Chaythoos by the Squamish (latitude 49.310 N | longitude 123.138 W).

He is remembered with a bronze bust sculpted by Charles Marega, a traditionally trained Italian sculptor. The bust is at the Beach Avenue entrance to the park, set on a column in a patch of lawn between the cycling path and Beach Avenue.

"The original budget for the project was $50,000," states Vancouver's Public Art Registry, referring to the original plan for a memorial gate, "but by the time Marega was commissioned in 1910, the project had become a bust for $4500, of which Marega was paid $3600 and the balance paid for an elaborate unveiling ceremony."[2]

I would like to say that the trees placed around the Oppenheimer commemorative bust have lived on. But like many trees planted in the park for specific purposes, such as providing a setting for a sculpture, they have been removed and replaced by others; sometimes the others are more in keeping with the times.

In this early photograph of the Oppenheimer bust, a monkey puzzle tree (*Araucaria araucana*) peeps out from behind the bust. It's a big tree, so although the archival record says the photograph was taken in 1911, it seems more likely it was taken after the tree had become established. Or it could be the tree was already established when the bust was set on its column. Anyhow, the monkey puzzle tree is long gone (see more in chapter 32).

Already in an 1980s photograph, a typically shaggy full-grown western redcedar provided the backdrop to the bust.

The trees that live on to the west and south of this bust opposite the Vancouver Park Board offices are native trees, growing where their seeds fell. The ornamental trees have been planted.

These planted trees function as an informal continuation of the row of planted large-leaf lindens, horse chestnuts, maples, and London plane trees that separate Stanley Park Drive from English Bay Beach.

Set in a flower bed facing the bust is an ornamental crabapple (*Malus*), its tiny, sour fruit giving away its common name. Beside it to the south, between the cycling path and the seawall, is an airy cluster that includes a colossal maple; a tall maple (which might be a bigleaf maple); an American beech, with its branches growing low to the ground and providing much shade; two mature paper birches, one with 2-inch catkins and the other with much smaller catkins and leaves; and, near the seawall, a European ash (*Fraxinus excelsior* 'Jaspidea') that turns a bright yellow every fall.

A thicket of cotoneaster shades the staircase down to the seawall. Thousands of red berries stand out gorgeously during drab winter days.

Oppenheimer is in good company.

Now in the 2020s, two groups of young western redcedars (three in each group) stand at Oppenheimer's shoulders, like protective guards. They haven't been there long.

TOP The bronze bust memorializing Mayor Oppenheimer nestles between a crabapple tree, six young western redcedars, and one mature western redcedar.

BOTTOM *Cotoneaster salicifolius* in the snow.

16

Gardens at the Pavilion

Oh, to be in England now that April's there,
And whoever wakes in England sees, some morning, unaware,
That the lowest boughs and the brushwood sheaf
Round the elm-tree bole are in tiny leaf,
While the chaffinch sings on the orchard bough
In England—now!

"Home Thoughts from Abroad," Robert Browning (1812–1889)

"HOME THOUGHTS FROM Abroad" is a poem Robert Browning wrote while vacationing in Italy in 1845. Clearly, Browning missed his homeland, but the next year he and his wife moved to Italy for her health. He probably grew his favourite English plants in his Italian garden, in the same way hundreds of thousands of immigrants to colonial Canada brought their plants and trees and planted them near to remind them of home. This was a formative period in Stanley Park's history and it is no surprise that many of the park's ornamental and shade-tree plantings reflect the longings of those who had left behind their native lands.

Between Salmon Stream Valley in the east and Pipeline Road in the west are three distinct gardens—the Rock Garden (begun in 1911), the gardens below Stanley Park Pavilion (built in 1911), and the Rose Garden (first planted in 1920).

As soon as builders began clearing away rocks and earth to lay foundations for the Stanley Park Pavilion in 1911, John Montgomery, a master gardener, took those rocks and boulders and repurposed

◄ OPPOSITE Stanley Park Pavilion sports a new roof following repairs in the winter of 2017–18.

Stanley Park Rock
Garden in 1916.

them for a rockery—a rock garden—to be
enjoyed by all. This photograph shows the
progress Montgomery had made by 1916.

Today, a rock-mounted plaque reads,

STANLEY PARK ROCK GARDEN

The first public garden of the city was created
from 1911 to 1920 by master gardener John
Montgomery from unwanted boulders excavated
for the adjacent park pavilion. Stretching from
Pipeline Road to Coal Harbour this early park
attraction had by the early 1950s become partially
abandoned, its story forgotten until revealed by
the devastating windstorm of December 15, 2006.
SPONSORED BY: CHRIS HAY / CANADA / VANCOUVER 125
VANCOUVERHERITAGEFOUNDATION.ORG

On the edge of the Rock Garden is a tree
with a plaque. This planting started a custom of Rotary Club presidents planting trees
of friendship when they visited other countries.[1] Sydney A. Pascall was visiting from
his home in London, England.

This tree was planted by

Sydney A. Pascall, President of Rotary

International Commemorating his visit

to Vancouver, June 15th, 1932

Intriguingly, this plaque is rather far
from the particular tree it's referencing,
making one unsure which tree to connect
with the plaque. The specimen, however,
turns out to be a beautiful, very tall, and
very rugged evergreen Japanese false cedar
(*Cryptomeria japonica* 'Lobbii'), a member of
the cypress family. One way to know you've
found it is by looking for an array of knobby
growths under one of its low branches, the
one that's bent upward like an arm at the

elbow. The very short, curved needles grow singly; their pointed ends are soft.

In July 2018, when I photographed this tree, both male and female cones looked dry. The male pollen cones grow together in round clusters, making them look like larger cones. Japanese cedar is known as *sugi* in Japan and is hugely popular for both its beauty while growing and its wood once logged. This popularity is despite the fact that the tree's pollen is a major cause of hay fever in Japan.[2]

Two Nootka cypress trees (*Chamaecyparis nootkatensis*, also known as *Cupressus nootkatensis*), also known as yellow cedar, grow in front of the Stanley Park Pavilion. They were planted in the early 1980s, one on each side of a westerly staircase, after the covered balcony area was enclosed. Boat builders favour yellow cedar because of its resistance to weather and water, its ability to yield a smooth finish, and its even yellow coloration. Where redcedar might be a carpenter's choice of wood above the water line, yellow cedar is the choice for below. It's interesting that neither of these "cedars" is actually in the Cedrus family.

A Pacific yew (*Taxus brevifolia*) tree grows near the east-west trail from the southeast corner of the Stanley Park Pavilion. Its trunk is rosy in places where the old bark has peeled away. Beware its poisonous seeds, hidden inside those fleshy red arils; indeed, every part of the plant is poisonous, except the aril.

TOP This rugged evergreen Japanese false cedar (*Cryptomeria japonica* 'Lobbii,' known in Japan as *sugi*) was planted in 1932.

BOTTOM Crowds gather at the original bandstand on a Sunday afternoon.

In the 1890s, concerts were held at the first bandstand, which had been set up just west of the current-day Information Booth parking lot, affording a view of Burrard Inlet. Once the pavilion was finished, a new bandstand was also built; now people had somewhere to eat and drink before and after the concerts.

Stanley Park was *the* place to celebrate such momentous events as the end of the First World War. It was where the Great Peace Celebration and Thanksgiving service took place on July 19, 1919, in front of the pavilion.

A view of the bandstand and pavilion around 1928 shows some of the mature trees already in evidence. I suspect that one of the seven in the foreground is the massive English elm that is there now. If this elm is an *Ulmus minor* 'Sarniensis,' I truly have to wonder how large an *U. major* would grow. Maybe *major* and *minor* refer to leaf size rather than tree size.

◀ OPPOSITE   Crowds gather below the Stanley Park Pavilion in 1917.

ACROSS BOTH PAGES   A Great Peace Celebration and Thanksgiving service took place on July 19, 1919, in front of the Stanley Park Pavilion.

ABOVE   Mature trees below the Stanley Park Pavilion in 1928.

The tallest deciduous tree in the image is the English elm (*Ulmus minor* 'Sarniensis'), though the giant Douglas-fir that lost its leader (to the right of the elm) is still the tallest tree around, according to the bald eagles.

This elm is just north of the Harding memorial sculpture, the most expensive memorial in the park. Built to commemorate the visit of US president Warren G. Harding to Canada, the statues, wall, and two engraved plaques were something of a shrine, as President Harding died a week after visiting Stanley Park in July 1923. He had already made history by being the first American president to visit Canada. The Kiwanis Club assessed its North American continent members fifty cents each to pay the winner of the memorial competition—Italian-born Charles Marega—to create a suitable memorial.[3]

The area below the pavilion always displays colourful flowers. Park Board gardening staff change the plants in the flower beds seasonally.

For the list of the trees in this chapter, I am indebted to Bill Stephen, Vancouver Park Board's Superintendent of Urban Forestry, for his chapter "Ornamental Trees of Stanley Park" in *Wilderness on the Doorstep*. As Bill warned me that some of the trees in his map had died, I looked for each tree, removed some from his list, and added some young ones that will be standouts in the years to come. He also explained that the rows of Corsican pines (*Pinus nigra* subsp. *laricio*, also known as Austrian black pines, which are at the top of this list; latitude 49.2985 N | longitude 123.1346 W) were planted behind the Stanley Park Zoo to create an attractive backdrop for photographs. Henry Avison, first park ranger, began that zoo when he caught and tethered a single black bear near his house; later he built a bear pit and added more bears and other animals. The zoo is now long gone.

The part of the park southwest of the first three and the last six on the list is known as the Rose Garden. Across Pipeline Road, in the extension of the Rose Garden, is a plaque that tells it all.

KIWANIS CLUB ROSE PLOT
First planted in 1920 to demonstrate the possibilities of rose culture in Vancouver "The City Beautiful"

▶ OPPOSITE TOP Theatregoers picnic in the pavilion grounds until the Theatre Under the Stars performance begins.

OPPOSITE BOTTOM *Gunnera* in the Stanley Park Pavilion pond and western redcedars around it.

Gardens at Stanley Park Pavilion

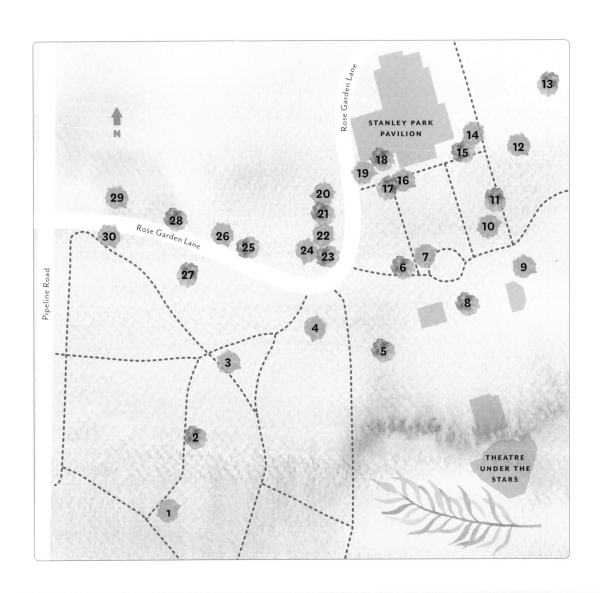

1. Two rows of Corsican pine (*Pinus nigra* subsp. *laricio*), a.k.a. Austrian black pine

2. Western redcedar (*Thuja plicata*) (there are several throughout this area)

3. Norway spruce (*Picea abies*)

4. Himalayan cedar (*Cedrus deodara*), a.k.a. deodar cedar

5. Bigleaf maple (*Acer macrophyllum*)

6. Katsura (*Cercidiphyllum japonicum*)

7. Saucer magnolia (*Magnolia × soulangeana*)

8. Rancho cherry (*Prunus sargentii* 'Rancho')

9. English elm (*Ulmus minor* 'Sarniensis')

10. Splitleaf maple (*Acer palmatum* var. dissectum)

11. Black tupelo (*Nyssa sylvatica*)

12. Pacific yew (*Taxus brevifolia*)

13. Japanese false cedar (*Cryptomeria japonica* 'Lobbii'), a.k.a. *sugi*

14. Chinese photinia (*Photinia serrulata*)

15. Eddie's White Wonder dogwood (*Cornus florida × C. nuttallii*)

16. Star magnolia (*Magnolia stellata*)

17. Harry Lauder's walking stick (*Corylus avellana* 'Contorta')

18. Nootka cypress (*Cupressus nootkatensis*, a.k.a. *Chamaecyparis nootkatensis*), a.k.a. yellow cedar

19. Upright Scots pine (*Pinus sylvestris* 'Fastigiata')

20. Lawson cypress (*Chamaecyparis lawsoniana*)

21. Sawara false cypress (*Chamaecyparis pisifera* 'Squarrosa')

22. Wisselii Lawson cypress (*Chamaecyparis lawsoniana* 'Wisselii')

23. Norway spruce (*Picea abies*)

24. Plumose Sawara false cypress (*Chamaecyparis pisifera* 'Plumosa')

25. Golden locust (*Robinia pseudoacacia* 'Frisia')

26. Golden Lawson cypress (*Chamaecyparis lawsoniana* 'Stewartii')

27. Sumac (*Rhus*)

28. Persian silk tree (*Albizia julibrissin*), a.k.a. pink silk tree and mimosa

29. Chinese witch hazel (*Hamamelis mollis*)

30. Dawyck beech (*Fagus sylvatica* 'Dawyck,' pronounced *doyk*)

FROM LEFT TO RIGHT

A young Norway spruce shows off its developing cones.

Seed cones on plumose Sawara false cypress (*Chamaecyparis pisifera* 'Plumosa') are shaped like small soccer balls (or "peas," hence their Latin species name *pisifera*). Pollen cones are barely visible.

A bob of drupes (stone fruit) begins to develop on sumac (*Rhus*).

Bigleaf maple samaras.

The area hosts over 3,500 rose bushes, an arbour covered with climbing roses, and this plaque:

VANCOUVER BOARD OF PARKS AND RECREATION

1888 Centennial Plaque 1988

Unveiled June 19th, 1988

"In celebration of 100 years of community service"

Park Commissioners

Malcolm Ashford, Chairman

Allan Bennett, Nancy A. Chiavario,

Andy Livingstone, Christopher Richardson,

Rolly Skov, George Wainborn

V. Kondrosky, General Manager

1893 / 1993

To commemorate the occasion of the Vancouver Pioneers' Association Centenary, this rose arbour and cairn are dedicated to the memory of all Vancouver pioneers.

Sincere appreciation for their generosity is extended to our late pioneer member Rector F. Steele, the Vancouver Park Board, the Provincial Government.

The cairn, containing historic Vancouver memorabilia, is to be opened October 26, 2093.

Will you be there?

TOP   A blush-pink rose starts to lose its petals.

BOTTOM   The trellis in the Rose Garden is a beautiful place for weddings, graduation photographs, and fashion shoots.

17

English Oaks for Shakespeare

*I want you to find the image, the memory of a tree that you know, a tree
that knows you. It could be any kind of tree. It could be an oak tree.
It could be an oak tree that attracts and survives the lightning and
holds onto its leaves longer than other deciduous trees.*

Robert Moss, author of *Dreaming the Soul Back Home* and *Mysterious Realities*

FOR ME, I DIDN'T only think of an oak. When I followed this
direction by Robert Moss, dream shaman, by dreaming in October
2017 of trees, I was swept away with images of some of the trees in
Stanley Park. At the time, I had already spent a month researching
the history of the entire park, and my book was already becoming
unwieldy. My tree dream made me realize I didn't have to write about
the entire park, because the history of the trees alone tells the park's
history. I changed course.

Do you remember the western redcedar that has half a dozen
stories to tell? It's the one at the eastern edge of the Shakespeare and
Perennial Garden, west of Pipeline Road, below the Rose Garden.

By sitting on one of the benches around that redcedar, we can see
the English oak (*Quercus robur*) that Mrs. Jonathan Rogers planted in
1916 on the tercentenary of William Shakespeare's death on April 23,
1616. That oak has grown into a giant during the last hundred years.

Devotees of the Bard of Avon formed the Vancouver Shakespeare
Society in 1916 to "promote enjoyment of Shakespeare's works through
readings, lectures, recitations and theatrical performances."[1]

Visibly rounded lobes on
English oak leaves.

Mrs. Jonathan Rogers planted an English oak (*Quercus robur*) in 1916 on the tercentenary of William Shakespeare's death.

The society was active for over sixty years, until 1979.

This small triangle of land where the first oak was planted became home to three more trees, this time commemorating actors, only one of them Shakespearean.

This tree "Comedy" was planted by the well known actress Eva Moore.

13th January 1921

Born in Brighton, England, in 1868, Eva Moore began her life on the stage at the age of nineteen. Over the next six decades, she performed in London in countless plays and later in film. She was an active suffragist, attending meetings and appearing in plays and films that supported the suffragist message of gender equality. In the early 1920s, she and her husband, actor and playwright Henry V. Esmond, travelled to Canada, performing the play *Eliza Comes to Stay: A Farce in Three Acts*, a comedy Esmond had written for his wife and himself.[2]

The Beginnings of the Shakespeare Garden

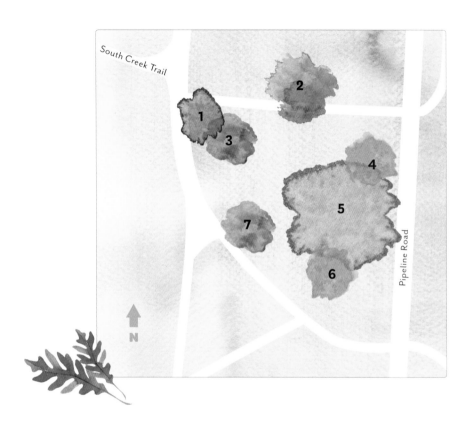

1. English oak (*Quercus robur*) "Tragedy"
2. Western redcedar with half a dozen stories to tell (*Thuja plicata*)
3. John Drainie dogwood tree (*Cornus nuttallii*)
4. Western redcedar (*Thuja plicata*)
5. English oak planted for the tercentenary of Shakespeare's death (*Quercus robur*)
6. Pacific yew (*Taxus brevifolia*)
7. English oak (*Quercus robur*) "Comedy"

All these years later, I think about the ceremony that would have attended the planting of Eva Moore's "Comedy" English oak. I expect there was lots of laughter. The oak is growing well.

A week and a half later, another English actor planted another English oak in the same plot of parkland.

And here we have the contrast. Whereas Eva Moore was a comedienne, Sir John Martin-Harvey (he hyphenated his surnames after being knighted earlier in 1921) was known by some as "the last of the great romantic actors."[3] At the time he planted the third English oak in Stanley Park, he and his wife, actress Nina de Silva, were touring Canada in their adaptation of Charles Dickens's *A Tale of Two Cities*, titled *The Only Way*.[4] Martin-Harvey was apparently acclaimed in Canada rather than in the US, and outside London rather than in London's West End. He was known as the "King of the Provinces,"[5] a moniker that worked in both Canada and the United Kingdom.

Forty-five years went by before a fourth commemorative tree was planted here, this time for a Canadian.

John Drainie, who began his career in Vancouver, performed on stage and in film, but he was best known for his performances in radio plays—Orson Welles called him "the greatest radio actor in the world."[6] He died at the young age of fifty, but he is remembered through the biography *Living the Part: John Drainie and the Dilemma of Canadian Stardom*, written by his broadcaster daughter, Bronwyn Drainie, and by two acting awards, ACTRA's John Drainie Award[7] and the Writers' Trust of Canada's Drainie-Taylor Biography Prize.[8] As well, he has a Star Walk plaque on Granville Street, at one time the hub of Vancouver's theatre district, and this tree in Stanley Park.

The tree that was planted more than fifty years ago for fifty-year-old Drainie is, appropriately, a Pacific dogwood (*Cornus nuttallii*)—the dogwood flower is the symbol of BC. Sadly, however, this particular dogwood seems to be suffering from a blight called *dogwood anthracnose*, a dogwood virus common on the West Coast. I am hopeful it will recover, in the same way that radio drama seems to be on the rise after a period of languishing.

18

Trees around Lost Lagoon

Trees carry the gaze upwards.

Coast of Many Faces, Catherine Kerr and Ulli Steltzer

THE FIRST CROSSING to Stanley Park was a very tall fallen Douglas-fir, along with many large boulders (as described in chapter 5, "The First Primitive Crossing").

The next crossing was a wooden bridge that Pauline Johnson, Chief Joe Capilano,[1] and others were able to canoe under (chapter 7, "The Big Fir"). The waters of Coal Harbour came and went, leaving intertidal mudflats—Pauline Johnson's Lost Lagoon. Members of the Vancouver Rowing Club also enjoyed going through the bridge opening during their training.

By 1910 plans were well under way to improve access to the park.

The crossing that followed the wooden bridge is the one there now, though it has been through a few iterations. Known as "the causeway," its construction began in 1916. Huge progress had been made by November 6, 1917 (remember the photograph on page 56?). Already, Coal Harbour's intertidal waters, which used to flow into Lost Lagoon, could flow no longer.

The Park Board replaced the salty ocean water that remained to the west of the causeway with fresh water, and Lost Lagoon became permanent, always "found." Water from the city's supply in Ceperley Meadow tops up the constantly declining water level in the lagoon. An outflow at the eastern end usually keeps out any saline inflow

from Coal Harbour, so the water seldom becomes brackish.

Meanwhile, the lagoon's natural flora changed from saltwater plants to freshwater ones. Local fish, birds, and small mammals changed too. Lost Lagoon is now a freshwater lake that provides natural habitat to local fauna plus a variety of migrating birds using the Pacific Flyway.

I will describe some of my favourite trees around Lost Lagoon. On the path along the most easterly part of the shore is a stunningly beautiful young Douglas-fir (latitude 49.2966 N | longitude 123.1368 W). Its first branches are unusually low to the ground. In summer it is dripping with cones, both green and mature.

On the east and south shores of Lost Lagoon are many flowing weeping willows,

◀ OPPOSITE, CLOCKWISE FROM TOP LEFT

A red-flowering currant (*Ribes sanguineum*).

A sumac bob is getting tall.

Beavers prefer to fell deciduous trees.

A community garden and tennis courts above Lost Lagoon.

New and old cones on a prolific Douglas-fir (*Pseudotsuga menziesii*) growing near path around Lost Lagoon.

TOP RIGHT Flowers emerge in January on a witch hazel shrub.

MIDDLE RIGHT Weeping willows on Lost Lagoon's southerly shore in summer.

BOTTOM RIGHT Flowing weeping willows along the Lost Lagoon path at the end of fall.

probably *Salix* 'Chrysocoma,' a species recognized by its yellow stems. They are healthy specimens that provide shade and protection for the many native (and invasive) small plants that border the lagoon's peripheral path.

Along the popular southwesterly path that borders the Stanley Park Pitch & Putt course—called the Azalea Walk (see pages 222 and 226 in chapter 30, "Ted and Mary Greig Rhododendron Garden")—is an abundance of gorgeous trees, many of them gigantic and well established. My favourites here are the ginkgoes, sequoias, magnolias, dogwoods, beeches, pines, and *Gunnera*. I'm not even mentioning the rhododendrons and

◀ OPPOSITE, CLOCKWISE FROM TOP LEFT

Lost Lagoon abuts the city.

Part of the biofiltration pond at dusk.

A distinctive tree on Lost Lagoon's east shore.

Several large beech trees dominate the southerly path between Lost Lagoon and some tennis courts.

TOP RIGHT The path beside Lost Lagoon.

BOTTOM RIGHT Waterfowl pond in the rain.

azaleas planted in the 1960s (see chapter 30). The walking path parallels the cycling path here; both are always busy.

Several paths come together at a cement bridge at the northerly end of Azalea Walk (latitude 49.2956 N | longitude 123.1461 W). At the natural waterfowl pond, a clearly recognizable beaver lodge slows the flow of the city's water into Lost Lagoon. I've seen herons, raccoons, turtles, wood ducks, mallards, and geese here. On one occasion, I watched a raccoon stealthily creep along a log upon which rested half a dozen mallards. I expect that pond is like visiting a fast food joint for raccoons—they will always be assured of a quick meal. The picture from that day is still in my mind's eye, though not, unfortunately, in a photograph.

There is a lovely specimen of western larch (*Larix occidentalis*) on the north side, about halfway around Lost Lagoon. Larches

Lost Lagoon.

are unusual in that they are deciduous conifers. They grow cones (3 to 5 centimetres long) *and* each fall they lose all their short needles (3 to 5 centimetres long and growing in tufts of 15 to 30). Which teaches me that not all conifers are evergreen.

The answer could be "larch" if you read the question in a crossword puzzle, "Which conifer is not an evergreen?"

19

Trees along the Seawall

*The trees seemed to march seaward still, going steadily over
the heights and down to the water's edge.*

The Country of the Pointed Firs, Sarah Orne Jewett (1849–1909)

FOUR YEARS INTO his long reign as superintendent of parks—from 1913 until 1936—W.S. Rawlings shared his idea of building a seawall to completely encircle Stanley Park. This was additional to Park Drive. It was partly intended to prevent erosion of the shoreline, but also to provide enjoyment to park goers. It has proved to be one of Stanley Park's most popular attractions among its 8 million annual visitors.

The work began in October 1917 with James Cunningham in charge. Known to his friends as Jimmy, Cunningham was an experienced Scottish master stonemason in his late thirties. He dedicated the rest of his life to this work for the next thirty-two years, tackling some of the toughest, sheer rock terrain along the west and north shores. Work took place in the evenings and at night to coincide with low tides. A plaque remembering Cunningham's work is embedded in the rock face beside the seawall south of Siwash Rock (latitude 49.3084 N | longitude 123.156 W).

Conflicts arose between walkers and cyclists initially; then it was decided each group should have its own separate path. Eventually, the cycle path became one-way, counter-clockwise.

The Annual James Cunningham Seawall Race began in October 1970 before the cycle path was complete. Finally, the seawall was

CLOCKWISE FROM TOP LEFT

This patterning on the bark of a western redcedar along the seawall intrigued me. I wondered whether this might be a culturally modified tree (a CMT). But checking with someone more in the know, I learned the pattern is more likely to have been left after an invasive plant (perhaps English ivy) was pulled away.

An elm seed has found footing in the seawall. Note the corky wings on the English elm's branches, grown to discourage any passing goats from chewing on its young shoots.

A stand of western redcedars along the seawall.

considered finished as a pedestrian-and-cyclist pathway in 1980, almost sixty-three years after the work had begun. It is now an 8.8-kilometre (5.5-mile) ride, run, walk, or jog. It currently connects the Canada Place Sails in Coal Harbour to the east with Kitsilano Beach Park to the south for a total of 19.8 kilometres (12.3 miles).

All along the seawall, there are both native trees and shrubs to appreciate and photograph, and some ornamental escapes to admire. For instance, a field elm sapling is growing courageously in the space between the cement blocks in the seawall. The opportunistic seed must originally have caught flight on a north wind from the field elm (*Ulmus minor* 'Sarniensis') growing 250 metres north, where it overlooks the President Harding sculpture.

Along the seawall, arborists, botanists, and nature photographers can get much

closer to some of the native evergreen giants such as Douglas-firs, western redcedars, and western hemlocks. Deep in the forest, these trees are competing in their race for the sun, self-pruning their lower limbs because they are in such close proximity with their neighbours. This sometimes makes their foliage hard to see. Along the seawall, it's a different matter. One such example grows north of Lumberman's Arch (latitude 49.3062 N | longitude 123.1339 W), a western hemlock that displays its small cones at head height.

Native deciduous and evergreen trees and shrubs growing along the way include vine maple (*Acer circinatum*), beeches, big-leaf maple (*Acer macrophyllum*), red alder (*Alnus rubra*), salal (*Gaultheria shallon*), snowberry (*Symphoricarpos albus*), Labrador tea (*Rhododendron groenlandicum*), and thimbleberry (*Rubus parviflorus*).

As I walk around the seawall, I hear crows and gulls. Canada geese call to each other, planning their next flight. Large and small flocks of Barrow's goldeneyes (black-and-white diving ducks) gather in English Bay. Various watery places in Stanley Park provide seasonal homes for the many migratory birds on the Pacific Flyway. Flotillas of wood ducks and mallards come closer in shore. A lone heron waits patiently for its next meal. The view along the seawall changes with every season.

A walk or a ride on the seawall goes past several Stanley Park landmarks and attractions that are not viewed from anywhere else, whether a person starts the seawall at marker 0 miles/km on the Promenade (the Georgia Street entrance) or at marker 9.0 km at the westerly seawall entrance from English Bay Beach. Going counter-clockwise, the

FROM LEFT TO RIGHT
Vine maple
(*Acer circinatum*).

The bark on a beech tree shows signs of age and earlier carvings.

A fruiting European beech on the seawall.

Edible salal berries are ripening.

◀ OPPOSITE, CLOCKWISE FROM TOP LEFT

The seawall in winter.

A couple of mature sweetgums (*Liquidambar styraciflua*) beside the seawall turn a burgundy red in fall.

A view of Vancouver, Coal Harbour, Stanley Park, and the seawall from Lions Gate Bridge.

Visitors look across Coal Harbour toward the HMCS *Discovery* naval base and the downtown skyline.

sights include the Royal Vancouver Yacht Club, the gates to HMCS *Discovery* on Deadman's Island, Hallelujah Point, the Harry Jerome statue, the Nine O'Clock Gun, the HMS *Egeria* benchmark, the Port of Vancouver viewpoint, and Brockton Point Lighthouse.

Turning to go north, the landmarks include the Chehalis Cross, the plaque to Captain Edward Stamp, the *Girl in a Wetsuit* statue, the *Empress of Japan* figurehead (a fibreglass replica), Prospect Point Lighthouse and the Prospect Point lookout, and Ferguson Point.

Retired in 1874 after thirty-eight years of BC coastal service with the Hudson's Bay Company, the English-built steamship *Beaver* became a towboat with the British Columbia Towing and Transportation Company. Under an inebriated crew and in strong tidal currents, the *Beaver* ran aground (1888) and finally sank (1892). From 1888 until

TOP   A path slopes up from the seawall.

BOTTOM   A view of the North Shore.

Before the two leaders broke off, this red alder held a record in Canada.

1926, when the light station was electrified, keeper John Grove made navigation around this headland safer with a beacon and fog bell at Prospect Point. The current lighthouse was built in 1948. When I visited Vancouver from Wales in 1961, I purchased a metal memento of SS *Beaver*. Little did I know . . .

The offshore views from the seawall are ever changing, of the Port of Vancouver, the North Shore, the Strait of Georgia (and Vancouver Island and islands in the Strait on a clear day), waiting port traffic, Pacific Spirit Regional Park and the University of British Columbia's Endowment Lands, West Point Grey, Kitsilano, and downtown Vancouver.

The second-largest red alder (*Alnus rubra*) in Canada overlooks Third Beach. It took me a while to find it because I began my search in the fall, when there were no leaves to help me. I finally recognized it by matching the path beside it to an older photograph. If I hadn't known it was a record tree, I wouldn't have noticed it there, to the right of the stairs and the concession stand, overlooking the beach and ocean.

Park goers walk the seawall, while freighters wait in Burrard Inlet for their turn to unload and reload in Vancouver's port.

Sit down and enjoy the sea view and the ambience of the forest.

Looking at its crown from a distance, I see that both its tall leaders have broken off. With them, it would indeed have been incredibly tall. But looking at it from afar when it is in leaf, what I admire is its spread, far over the bank on one side and across the path on the other.

It is a tree that some think has resulted from the merging of several younger, smaller trees. And if that were not so, it might have come first. I don't believe the tree cares! It is enjoying its time in the sun, master of all it surveys.

If the tide is out and you have on some non-slip shoes, you may want to explore the intertidal zone, rich with rockweed, marine algae, barnacles, and mussels. However, step carefully because the rocky areas (not the beaches) are considered by Stanley Park Ecology Society (see chapter 32) to be Environmentally Sensitive Areas. Despite the constant ocean-going traffic, forests of bull kelp on the east side provide safe habitat for many marine species of fish.

20

Growing Together

The definition of a tree is not always clear-cut. There is no problem saying that big trees with single trunks are definitely trees, while small, bushy plants with several trunks and limbs down to the ground are shrubs, but where does one stop and the other start?

Trees of Vancouver, Gerald B. Straley

A Thick Skin Comes with Age

AS A TREE grows in height, it also grows in girth. Year by year, it adds another ring to its heartwood, the wood accumulating inside the cambium layer, from the xylem. The first spurt of woody growth happens every spring, when the tree wakes up to the longer hours of daylight, the increased strength of the sun, and its new leaves' ability to photosynthesize more energy from the sunlight. This first spring growth spurt shows up as a dark-coloured layer of wood. As the new wood proliferates through the year, slowing down in the drier, hotter months of summer, the additional cells become less dense and thus lighter in colour.

This annual ring, comprising darker and lighter areas, helps us age a tree precisely. For instance, scientists working with entomologist Dr. George McGavin on the BBC documentary *Oak Tree: Nature's Greatest Survivor* were able to determine that the earliest timber used to construct the entirety of Salisbury Cathedral and its spire—the tallest in Britain—came from oak trees felled in the spring of 1222.[1]

How astonishing that they were able to pin down the actual year! And yet, why not? We humans have been able to count for a long time.

But it's not that simple, because the scientists had to match the size of the growth rings on one piece of wood to the growth rings on wood whose age was known, and then overlap that knowledge with knowledge of others. The process of that calculation must be a story in itself.

The outer surface of the cambium layer of a tree's trunk, branches, stems, and roots—the phloem—transports the sugar solution created by the leaves to wherever it is required for growth.

Recently, a theory has been put forth regarding how nourishing energy moves within a tree. The tree relies on the way water molecules are linked together by their positive and negative charges. As a water molecule evaporates from a leaf, a vacuum is created that draws up the next water molecule, and the next. And so it is water's electrical properties that actually determine the maximum height of those trees that grow tall.[2] Nothing else. Oh, except the soil, the mycorrhizal networks, the environment, and the weather.

In many tree families, the outer bark (the part that is external to the phloem) grows a layer of cork to protect the tree from moisture loss, insect invasion, and infection from bacteria and fungi. The cork layer cuts off the external bark cells from all moisture and nourishment, and so they die. The external layer of bark is dead tissue, serving to protect the tree from drought, sunburn, fire, and frost.

This thick protective skin that evolves with age on a tree trunk (think of the thick grooves of a mature Douglas-fir) allows the tree to survive the toughest conditions while also providing a home to small mammals, birds, and insects.

Wisdom Comes with Age

In the same way that a tree grows a thick bark as it matures, so many of us humans grow a "thick skin" as we mature. With the wisdom of maturity, we learn to overlook insults and slights, forgive past wrongs, let go of regrets, and share what we have. We learn to recognize that sharing ourselves and our belongings actually increases what we have.

Communities of People

The behaviours attributed to trees by the two crown-shyness theories (in chapter 8) also seem to happen among people. Family members, friends, and colleagues frequently support each other, giving each person space to shine in their own particular way. Groups that work together, such as an orchestra, a rugby team, or a research team, behave in the same way, allowing each person to exercise their particular strengths for the benefit of all. When people in the same community do not overshadow each other, they allow each other to find their own place in the sun.

In addition, life knocks the rough spots off people. People talk about so-and-so being a "rough diamond." That person

Fallen, wet leaves have turned rose brown between the tree trunks.

needs to face a few dilemmas, be part of a tricky negotiation, and learn the ways of the world to smooth out differences rather than accentuate them. We want that person to experience a comeuppance, "for their own good."

There are many times when the crown-shyness attitude of trees is not exhibited by people. For instance, if a person in a public space starts talking loudly on their cellphone while everyone at the tables around them is chatting quietly, trying to mind their own business, it feels as though the cellphone person is imposing their self-importance on everyone around them. This is not a communal attitude.

Humans can learn much from the communal attitude of trees: live and let live.

21

Lumberman's Arch Avenue

Platanus × hispanica *is an interspecific hybrid. The parents are*
the European-Asian Platanus orientalis *(oriental plane) and the*
American P. occidentalis (sycamore, American plane, buttonwood)…
known to produce hybrids spontaneously when in close proximity.
Fertile seedlings are thought to have first arisen from cultivated
trees south of London, England, sometime before 1700,
whereupon the common name was coined.

Douglas Justice, Vancouver Trees app

I HAVE PORED over archival photographs with uncertain dates and wrong locations[1] to roughly establish the date and the reason why a 300-metre-long curved avenue of London plane trees (*Platanus × hispanica*) was planted at Lumberman's Arch in Stanley Park. The London plane is thought to be a hybrid of Oriental plane (*Platanus orientalis*) and American sycamore (*Platanus occidentalis*). The avenue itself went from the old pier near Lumberman's Arch to parts of the original Stanley Park Zoo.

I think I have figured out why and when this avenue of trees was planted, but this story is long. Bear with me.

I'll start in early 1912, seven years before the planting occurred, when loggers purposefully rolled up their sleeves and felled one colossally tall Douglas-fir with a trunk 4 feet (1.2 metres) in diameter. This hulk was trimmed into eight 18-foot (5.5-metre) lengths, so the original tree was well over 144 feet (44 metres) tall before it became slimmer in girth. Each section weighed over 5 tons (4.5 tonnes).[2]

Members of the British Columbia Lumber Manufacturers Association planned to erect an arch on Pender Street near Hamilton Street for the visit of the Duke and Duchess of Connaught and their daughter Princess Patricia on September 18, 1912. This was to be an arch made mostly of undressed logs rather than of finished lumber. In photographs taken during construction of the arch, the bark is clearly that of a Douglas-fir, with deep grooves typical of the species.

Men use crane and pulleys to erect Lumbermen's Arch on Pender Street near Hamilton Street in September 1912, for the upcoming visit of Duke of Connaught. Each log weighs 5 tons.

This was to be a triumphal arch, built for some of the same reasons that Romans built their triumphal arches:

1. To honour the visit of a prince. The Duke of Connaught, known better as Prince Arthur William Patrick Albert, was the seventh child and third son of Queen Victoria and Prince Albert. His nephew was the recently crowned King George V, monarch of the United Kingdom and the British Dominions.

2. To honour the visit of the Governor General of Canada. Prince Arthur, the Duke of Connaught, was also the first royal prince to be sworn in as Governor General of Canada, an event that had happened just the previous year, in 1911.

3. To honour the visit of an Honorary Regimental Colonel. The Duke of Connaught had assumed the position of Honorary Colonel of the Sixth Regiment, the Duke of Connaught's Own Rifles, on May 1, 1900.

4. To celebrate the dedication of a new bridge. The Duke of Connaught was here to dedicate the one-year-old Cambie Street Bridge, known for a short while as the Connaught Bridge.

Using pulleys and hoists and great determination, construction workers raised the 5-ton logs one by one into position, right there on Pender Street. Heave ho! Heave ho!

This was the first Lumbermen's Arch.

It was just one of *ten* elaborate ceremonial arches erected specifically for the three-day visit of the Duke and Duchess of Connaught and Princess Patricia. I find this so intriguing that I must give you the list of ten, alphabetically:[3]

1. Canadian Northern Railway arch at Hastings Street and Seymour Street

2. Chinese arch on Hastings Street at Pender Street and Carrall Street

3. City of Vancouver arch at Hastings Street and Granville Street

4. German, Swiss, and Austrian Societies' arch on Granville Street

5. Great Northern Railway arch on Hastings Street between Hamilton Street and Homer Street

6. Italian Colony arch on Hastings Street between Hamilton Street and Homer Street

7. Japanese arch at Hastings Street and Main Street

LEFT Lumbermen's Arch on Pender Street at Hamilton Street is festooned with greenery.

RIGHT Stanley Park arch at the Georgia Street entrance to the park. The sentinel big fir from chapter 7 towers over the Stanley Park arch to welcome Lord Connaught in 1912.

8. Lumbermen's Arch on Pender at Hamilton Street

9. Progress Club arch at Granville Street and Dunsmuir Street

10. Stanley Park arch at the Georgia Street entrance to the park

You will have noticed that Stanley Park erected an arch for the visit. What's that just behind the arch? Why, that's our sentinel big fir from chapter 7, "The Big Fir"!

The Duke and Duchess of Connaught and Princess Patricia travelled under this arch and beside the sentinel fir in a horse-drawn carriage. I expect they stopped for a few moments to pay homage at the memo-

rial to Queen Victoria, erected in the park six years earlier. (When I last passed by this simple monument—originally a drinking fountain, until a typhoid scare put a stop to the public's sharing the chained cups—a murder of crows in the maple that towers behind it was making a heck of a racket.)

Even though British Columbia had joined Canadian Confederation in 1871 and was therefore no longer a colony under direct British rule, Canada's most westerly province held fast to its British connections. It was proud of being *British* Columbia; the term "Dominion of Canada" had not yet fallen out of common use. People turned out in the thousands to welcome the royal family.

The Duke and Duchess and Princess Patricia continued on to Brockton Oval,

where a grand ceremonial march-past of troops took place. Enthusiastic crowds gathered at Brockton Point for the event.

A year after the British royal family returned home, Lumbermen's Arch was dismantled, floated through the harbour, and reinstalled in Stanley Park, to rest in the area that had been Whoi Whoi (currently known as Xway xway), the home of generations of Squamish, Musqueam, and Tsleil-Waututh people.[4] Lumbermen's Arch became a "trysting place," where lovers would carve their initials into the arch, inside a heart.

For a while the arch was known as the Bowie Arch, after its designer, Captain G.P. Bowie, who was killed at Ypres on July 7, 1915—one of 6,500 Canadians killed, wounded, or captured in that first major battle fought by Canadians in the First World War.

After being set up in its new location in Stanley Park, Lumbermen's Arch was dedicated on August 29, 1919. I believe that dedication occurred as an extension of the Great Peace Celebration and Thanksgiving service that had taken place in front of the Stanley Park Pavilion on July 19, 1919 (mentioned on page 107 in chapter 16, "Gardens at the Pavilion").

On September 22, 1919, a mere twenty-four days after the belated dedication of Lumbermen's Arch, Vancouver welcomed another member of the British royal family: Prince Edward, the Prince of Wales (later King Edward for a brief time, and later yet, the Duke of Windsor). Prince Edward was

LEFT Lumbermen's Arch resides in its Stanley Park location.

RIGHT People gather around the Prince of Wales arch on September 22, 1919, at the Georgia Street entrance to Stanley Park.

TOP Fruit on a London plane tree (*Platanus × hispanica*).

BOTTOM Himalayan white pine pollen cones (*Pinus wallichiana*) are developing in May.

grandson of Queen Victoria, son of King George V and Queen Mary, and nephew of the Duke of Connaught.

Like his uncle before him, the Prince of Wales was taken under an archway at the entrance to the park, across the newly established causeway crossing the Coal Harbour narrows. His itinerary included a welcome ceremony in the bandstand in Stanley Park, south of the Stanley Park Pavilion.

My hypothesis is that the Prince of Wales's trip to or from the ceremonies in the park's bandstand took him past the Lumbermen's Arch that had been built in 1912 for his uncle and moved to its new location. And the route took the prince through an avenue of newly planted London plane trees to commemorate his visit. These trees replaced the fencing that had lined a roadway leading from the arch to the Stanley Park Zoo. In searching around for proof of my theory, I found some intriguing photos, but maybe I've merely uncovered a coincidence, a whim of timing.

These London plane trees have grown into gnarly specimens that burst forth every spring with leaves, round red flowers and later fruit, provide shade in summer's heat, and trace hopeful branches across a blue or grey sky every winter.

On August 25, 1943, fifty-five years after being first opened, Stanley Park was rededicated ceremoniously at Lumbermen's Arch. Frank Plante, the man who had driven Lord and Lady Stanley and Mayor and Mrs. Oppenheimer to the original dedication fifty-five years earlier, drove E.V. Young and David Oppenheimer to Lumbermen's Arch in a horse-drawn carriage. Dressed in frock coats and top hats, David Oppenheimer played the part of Mayor David Oppenheimer, his great-uncle, while E.V. Young played the part of Lord Stanley. It is fitting that Young would play this role as he was the artistic director, stage manager, and actor for fifteen years (into the mid-fifties) with Theatre Under the Stars, the amateur dramatic company that still performs every summer in Malkin Bowl, south of Stanley Park Pavilion.

Northwest of the arch itself is a simple grove of three Himalayan white pines (*Pinus wallichiana*), discernible by their bundles of five long, softly drooping needles and their large cones measuring up to 20 centimetres long. Farther to the northwest, some showy Japanese maples provide a splash of fall colour to contrast with the local western redcedars.

As a postlude, that first Lumbermen's Arch stayed in its second location until it began to deteriorate. It was demolished on

▷ OPPOSITE TOP Colourful maples beside the concession stand at Lumberman's Arch.

OPPOSITE BOTTOM Blush-red leaves fall from a maple in November.

TOP Children climb aboard Lumberman's Arch in the 1970s. PUGSTEM PUBLICATIONS.

BOTTOM Summer at Lumberman's Arch.

December 3, 1947, when it was found to be suffering from dry rot. Five years later, in 1952, it was replaced (a little to the northeast of the original location) by a less ambitious arch of four large logs, one supported by the three others. Initially, this arch looked quite dramatic, but gradually four yew trees (three Pacific yews and one English yew) have grown over one end, obscuring the dramatic way the log on top seems ready to roll off its support. Perhaps that's also when Lumber*men*'s Arch changed its name almost everywhere to Lumber*man*'s Arch.

Ornamental Cherry Trees

Loveliest of trees, the cherry now
Is hung with bloom along the bough

A Shropshire Lad, Alfred Edward Housman

THE JAPANESE-CANADIAN WAR MEMORIAL in Stanley Park is a testament to the struggle that immigrant Japanese and Japanese Canadians have endured, living in Vancouver. The plaques on the memorial tell the story.

CENTENARY OF ENLISTMENT

Japanese Canadians were unable to enlist in BC at the onset of the Great War. Under the leadership of Yasushi Yamazaki, the Canadian Japanese Association sponsored the training of a heroic battalion of 227 men in Vancouver in January 1916. Undeterred by refusal from government and disbandment, the volunteers travelled at their own expense to Alberta to enlist one by one in May 1916. Determined to represent Canada. They were fearless in battle, inspiring the victory on Vimy Ridge and other battles identified on the granite petals of the cenotaph. These brave men were awarded thirteen military medals and two St. George Crosses.
National Association of Japanese Canadians

JAPANESE CANADIAN WAR MEMORIAL

This monument was dedicated on April 9, 1920 in lasting memory of more than 222 who answered the call of duty for Canada and to the 54 who

In Japan, the privilege of seeing a flowering cherry tree and picnicking under it was initially reserved for royalty. Over the years, members of noble families, those of senior military rank, and finally commoners were extended the privilege. These flowering cherry trees were hybridized stock, selected for their profusion of blossoms, their colour, and their early blooming. They were given the revered name of village cherries, *Sato Zakura*.

The avenue trees at the war memorial are village cherries—*Prunus* Sato Zakura Group 'Shirotae.' The sentinel is also a village cherry, a *Prunus* Sato Zakura Group 'Ojochin,' a rare tree that has lived long, growing from its roots (rather than being grafted). The 'Ojochin' grows large, hanging, lantern-shaped flowers in spring.

This photo of the Canadian Japanese Society at the Japanese-Canadian war memorial was taken twelve years after the memorial in Stanley Park was unveiled. A guardian village cherry tree is now growing beside the memorial. The date of this photograph is May 10, 1932,[1] five days before the assassination of the eighteenth prime minister of Japan. Is that a coincidence? Unrest in their native land had alerted these men.

By 1939, the 'Ojochin' had grown quite large, though not as large as the foreground 'Shirotae' avenue trees. These days, a century after the cenotaph was unveiled, the 'Ojochin' is a knobby, gnarled specimen

Photo taken in 1932 of the Canadian Japanese Society at the Japanese-Canadian war memorial shows the young *Prunus* Sato Zakura Group 'Ojochin.'

sacrificed their lives in defence of freedom in WWI. Engraved on the monument is the Honour Roll of WWI and those who lost their lives in WWI, WWII, the Korean War and the Afghan War.

A re-lighting of the memorial lantern, which was extinguished during WWII, took place on August 2, 1985 by WWI Veteran, Sgt. M. Mitsui MM.

At the time of the unveiling of the Japanese Canadian war memorial on April 9, 1920, the cenotaph seemed to have no trees around it, except for a Douglas-fir. Soon, an avenue and one special guardian tree were planted nearby—all of them ornamental flowering cherries.

whose two trunks have been bolted together and whose lowest branches have been cut back at various times for the safety of visitors to the shrine.

Immigrants have great influence on the culture of the country that becomes their new home. So strong has the influence of the Japanese people and their love of cherry trees as the herald of spring been that Canada's most westerly mainland city now celebrates the blossoming of ornamental cherry trees too, through the Vancouver Cherry Blossom Festival. The festival began in April 2005. The best guide to finding Vancouver's cherry trees is *Ornamental Cherries in Vancouver*, a 124-page book by Douglas Justice, associate director and curator of collections at the University of British Columbia Botanical Garden. Its third edition came out in 2014.

Japanese flowering cherry (*Prunus serrulata*) is Japan's unofficial national flower, beloved and treasured.

More than a quarter of the sidewalk trees in the West End (planted, maintained, and cared for by the Vancouver Park Board) are the *Prunus* genus. This genus includes almonds, apricots, nectarines, peaches, and plums, as well as cherries. Many of these sidewalk trees (almost eight hundred of them) are very pretty cherry plum trees (*Prunus cerasifera*), and many are Sargent cherry trees, also known as North Japanese hill cherry trees (*Prunus sargentii*). More

TOP The *Prunus* Sato Zakura Group 'Ojochin' in 1939 grows close to the memorial.

BOTTOM Armistice Day is remembered at the Japanese-Canadian war memorial on November 11, 2018. A few last leaves hang on to the 'Ojochin.'

than half of the *Prunus* trees in the West End are Japanese flowering cherries (*Prunus serrulata*). Their many flowers, which last throughout the month of April, are a delight.

City-wide, Vancouver is growing over nineteen thousand *Prunus*, almost a third of the city's entire abundance of sidewalk trees, which numbered 65,535 in October 2019.

Flowering cherry trees are quite delicate, especially since many are hybrids that have been grafted onto a wild cherry (*Prunus avium*). Grafting is a method of attaching a flowering young cultivar to a sturdy young rootstock, matching cambium layer to cambium layer. Disease can easily establish itself at a graft site. Some flowering cherries do not live more than two or three decades.

In Stanley Park, flowering cherries are growing well in several locations other than the war memorial.

· One tree of *Prunus serrulata* 'Snow Goose' grows in Ceperley Meadow, south of North Lagoon Drive. This is a white cultivar (a Dutch hybrid of Fuji cherry and Japanese hill cherry) that blooms in early April. Its leaves turn a deep peach colour in the fall.

· One *Prunus* Sato Zakura Group 'Shujaku' grows near the stone bridge over Ceperley Stream where it flows into Lost Lagoon. This is another rare cultivar. Its pale pink petals deepen into red.

◄ OPPOSITE The *Prunus* Sato Zakura Group 'Ojochin' planted as a sentinel at the Japanese-Canadian war memorial.

ABOVE *Prunus serrulata* 'Snow Goose' grows in Ceperley Meadow.

· Four or five *Prunus* Sato Zakura Group 'Gyoiko' grow on the north side of the Pitch & Putt, on both sides of the rail fence. The flowers of this cultivar sport a stripe of green

Pale pink blossoms of daybreak cherries
(*Prunus* × *yedoensis*) in mid-April.

Some of these cherry trees growing in the Shakespeare Garden might be ones donated to the Park Board by Mr. and Mrs. Uyeda.

in their petals, a rare feature in a blossom.

- One *P.* × *subhirtella* 'Atsumori' grows east of the Pitch & Putt entrance on Lagoon Drive. It flowers mid-April. Its leaves turn yellow and orange in the fall.

- Three *P.* × *subhirtella* 'Autumnalis Rosea' grow near the Pooh Corner Day Care at Lost Lagoon. This is a very early-flowering cultivar (as early as December in a mild winter). It is a pale pink variety.

In gratitude to their new home, a Japanese immigrant couple, Bunjiro and Kimi Uyeda, donated a thousand young cherry trees to the Park Board in August 1935, with the stipulation that Stanley Park get first priority. This was the first such donation. The trees were not planted out immediately, because the city was struggling to make ends meet during the tough 1930s and could not cover the wages required for the extra work. Two years later, some of the trees were planted out, but not all.

Then on September 10, 1939, Canada united with Great Britain in the Second

World War. On January 14, 1942, one month after the Japanese strike on Pearl Harbor, Prime Minister Mackenzie King ordered the removal of "all adult males of Japanese ancestry" from the West Coast.[2] Among the thousands of people and families who were relocated to BC's Interior and elsewhere in Canada were Mr. and Mrs. Uyeda and their three children. They moved to Montreal and never returned.

In April 1942, three months after the Uyeda family had been "removed" from Vancouver, seven hundred of their donated cherry trees were planted out, some of them in the Shakespeare Garden (chapter 27). They were now being called "Chinese cherry trees."

Mariko Uyeda was the middle child of Bunjiro and Kimi. She is remembered by her nieces and nephews in *Return: A Commemorative Yearbook in Honour of the Japanese Canadian Students of 1942*.[3] They remembered that their aunt had once said, "the imposed curfew was a terrible humiliation."[4]

Several more ornamental cherries that I know of were planted to the west of the Promenade slope. More grow beside the Ted and Mary Greig Rhododendron pathway from the tennis courts to the West End (chapter 30). They are rugged specimens that reveal little of their history. I pass them every time I walk to or from the Stanley Park Lawn Bowling Club, coming from a Friday evening barbecue or a Wednesday bridge afternoon. See chapter 30, "Ted and Mary Greig Rhododendron Garden," for more about the trees in this area.

When the cherry trees blossom in Vancouver, the cameras come out. Models pose under falling pink petals, couples have their wedding photographs taken, and ushers group together beside the groom.

23

A Putting Green
and a Sports Pavilion

So harmonious and finely balanced are even the mightiest of these monarchs in all their proportions that there is never anything overgrown or monstrous about them. Seeing them for the first time you are more impressed with their beauty than their size, their grandeur being in great part invisible; but sooner or later it becomes manifest to the loving eye, stealing slowly on the senses.

Description of *Sequoiadendron giganteum* in *The Yosemite*, John Muir

A PUTTING GREEN for Vancouver's golfers was laid out in 1920 on a triangle of lawn bordered by Stanley Park Drive on one side and Lagoon Drive on the other (latitude 49.2925 N | longitude 123.1474 W). The third side is now bounded by a walking path going northeast from Stanley Park Drive.

On the next page is a simple plan of the area this chapter covers. It includes the Stanley Park Lawn Bowling Club (SPLBC); the Oppenheimer Bust (OB; see chapter 15); and the Vancouver Park Board (VPB; see chapter 29).

This putting green began life during the period when W.S. Rawlings was managing the park's evolution and living in the Park Board's house at 2099 Beach Avenue. Having already served the board as secretary for some years, Rawlings refined the Park Board's volunteer approach to that of a professional organization. Serving on the board from 1913 to 1936, he was the longest-serving superintendent

Ubiquitous Canada geese graze near the avenue of horse chestnuts (*Aesculus hippocastanum*).

Named Spaces around
the Putting Green and Sports Pavilion

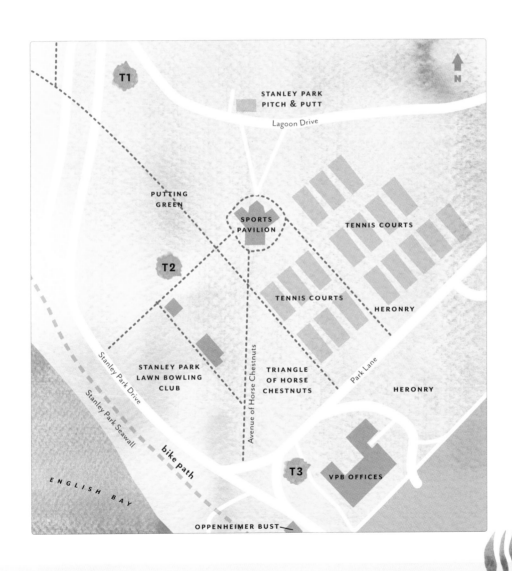

Page 158 describes the trees T1 to T3.

Nests in the heronry.

of parks. Rawlings is recognized as the early superintendent most influential in shaping the park to what it is today, and a popular trail is named after him.

Farther to the east of the putting green at that time were the first of the eighteen tennis courts that exist there now (there is another bank of four more courts overlooking Lost Lagoon from the south). The early courts must have been built by 1912, because in that year, according to Richard M. Steele's book *The First 100 Years: The Vancouver Board of Parks and Recreation; An Illustrated Celebration*, the Park Board padlocked the tennis courts to prevent their being used on Sundays in violation of the Lord's Day Act.

(This Lord's Day Act came into being in Canada in 1906, following a precedent set in England by the Sunday Observance Act of 1625. This had been at the beginning of the reign of Charles I, monarch of the three kingdoms of England, Scotland, and Ireland. Being Welsh, I am now wondering who the monarch of Wales was at the time, but that's another matter. Let's get back to the trees.)

Trees around the Putting Green and Sports Pavilion

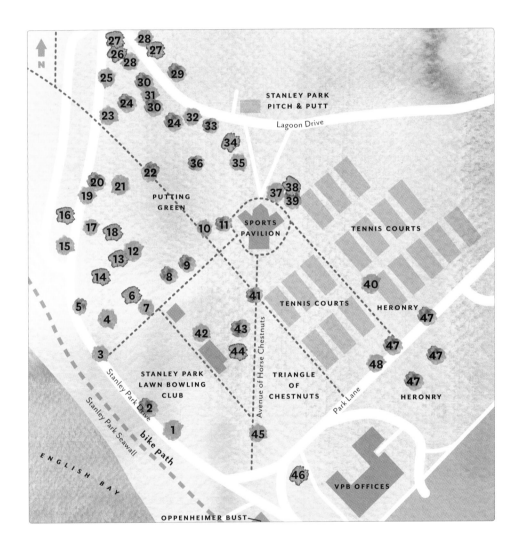

1. Variegated western redcedar (*Thuja plicata* 'Zebrina')

2. Douglas-fir (*Pseudotsuga menziesii*)

3. Himalayan cedar (*Cedrus deodara*), a.k.a. deodar cedar

4. Corkscrew willow (*Salix matsudana* 'Tortuosa'), young

5. Western redcedar (*Thuja plicata*)

6. Black pine (*Pinus nigra*)

7. Sawara false cypress (*Chamaecyparis pisifera* 'Squarrosa')

8. Bigleaf maple (*Acer macrophyllum*), planted for Jody Taylor

9. Tricolour beech (*Fagus sylvatica* 'Roseomarginata'), a.k.a. pink nightie beech

10. Three maples (*Acer*) and a western redcedar (*Thuja plicata*)

11. Harry Lauder's walking stick (*Corylus avellana* 'Contorta')

12. Black locust (*Robinia pseudoacacia*), young

13. Beech (*Fagus*)

14. Black locust (*Robinia pseudoacacia*), young

15. Norway maple (*Acer platanoides* 'Crimson King')

16. Japanese pagoda tree (*Sophora japonica*), a.k.a. scholar tree

17. Variegated sycamore maple (*Acer pseudoplatanus* 'Leopoldii')

18. Scarlet oak (*Quercus coccinea*)

19. Red alder (*Alnus rubra*)

20. Red buckeye (*Aesculus pavia*), a.k.a. red horse chestnut

21. Hungarian oak (*Quercus frainetto* 'Forest Green')

22. Silver maple (*Acer saccharinum*)

23. Bigleaf maple (*Acer macrophyllum*)

24. Norway spruce (*Picea abies*)

25. Western redcedar (*Thuja plicata*)

26. Queen Elizabeth English oak (*Quercus robur*)

27. Three Chinese red-bark birch (*Betula albosinensis* var. *septentrionalis*), two in one place and another on the other side of Lagoon Drive

28. Two maidenhair trees (*Ginkgo biloba*), one on either side of Lagoon Drive

29. Three Himalayan cedars (*Cedrus deodara*), a.k.a. deodar cedar, on the other side of Lagoon Drive

30. European hazelnut (*Corylus avellana*)

31. Two Norway spruce trees (*Picea abies*)

32. Giant sequoia (*Sequoiadendron giganteum*), a.k.a. Sierra redwood

33. Coast redwood (*Sequoia sempervirens*), a.k.a. California redwood

34. Incense cedar (*Calocedrus decurrens*)

35. Giant sequoia (*Sequoiadendron giganteum*), a.k.a. Sierra redwood

36. Western redcedar (*Thuja plicata*)

37. Catalpa × desert willow (*Chitalpa tashkentensis*)

38. Sawara false cypress (*Chamaecyparis pisifera* 'Squarrosa')

39. Plumose Sawara false cypress *Chamaecyparis pisifera* 'Plumosa')

40. A row of three maples and the rest are London plane trees (*Platanus × hispanica*)

41. Avenue of horse chestnuts (*Aesculus hippocastanum*)

42. Sawara cypress (*Chamaecyparis pisifera* 'Squarrosa'), a.k.a. Japanese false cypress

43. Himalayan cedar (*Cedrus deodara*)

44. Colorado blue spruce (*Picea pungens*)

45. Shagbark hickory (*Carya ovata*)

46. Red oak (*Quercus rubra*)

47. Heronry

48. A row of four English oaks (*Quercus robur*)

FROM TOP TO BOTTOM A red alder grows tall.

Close-up of Chinese red-bark birch (*Betula albosinensis* var. *septentrionalis*) in the putting green.

Another red-bark birch tree grows near the snake rail fence surrounding the Pitch & Putt course.

A curtain of red oak leaves almost hides the sports pavilion behind.

Many trees are of great interest in this plot of land encircled by Stanley Park Drive, Lagoon Drive, and the north-south avenue of horse chestnut trees. They are as follows:

· the putting green trees
· the horse chestnut avenue and triangle trees
· the heronry trees
· T1, the Queen Elizabeth Windsor oak (*Quercus robur*) within the group of putting green trees (26 on the map above)
· T2, the Jody Taylor maple (8 on the map above)
· T3, the red oak (*Quercus rubra*) at the corner of Park Lane and Beach Avenue near the Vancouver Park Board offices

Many of these trees, especially the California giants (32 to 35), are referred to in articles about Stanley Park. For the names of many of the cultivars in this region, I am once more indebted to Bill Stephen.[1] One of the ways I have learned how to identify trees is by comparing the leaves on this tree

FROM TOP TO BOTTOM

A western redcedar (part of it with variegated needles) towers over the Stanley Park Lawn Bowling Club.

Corkscrew willow leaves are unmistakable.

The Jody Taylor memorial bigleaf maple often has an ornament adorning it.

to the ones on that tree, by comparing the bark and the shape of this tree to the bark and the shape of that tree. As David Tracey said would happen, in *Vancouver Tree Book*, I have gradually started to recognize a tree by its whole rather than its parts.[2]

Let's start in front of the Stanley Park Lawn Bowling Club, originally an elk paddock at the time the putting green was first delineated. Close inspection of the western redcedar here reveals parts of it to be a 'Zebrina' cultivar, with gorgeous yellow stripes within the green foliage.

From here we move into the parkland area. These days, this large area shows no sign of having once been a putting green. Only the occasional map provides the evidence.

The putting green trees turn out to be a mixture of ages. Three young ones are a corkscrew willow (*Salix matsudana* 'Tortuosa') (4 on the map) and two black locusts (*Robinia pseudoacacia*) (12 and 14).

The next tree to recognize in this corner of the park is the Jody Taylor Memorial Tree (latitude 49.292 N | longitude 123.1472 W) (8 on the map). It's a bigleaf maple (*Acer macrophyllum*). City of Vancouver arborist Jody Taylor was trimming a catalpa tree in Connaught Park in the Kitsilano neighbourhood when the heavy branch he had just trimmed fell on him and killed him. Having worked for the Park Board for thirteen years, Jody was a great example of the dedicated men and women who tend the trees in the

A beautiful Japanese pagoda tree.

parks and along the streets and boulevards of this beautiful city.

Jody left behind a ten-year-old daughter named Tristen. An educational fund was set up for Tristen,[3] and a plaque on a park bench (near latitude 49.2921 N | longitude 123.1467 W) memorializes Jody:

He loved life and lived it his way.
In loving memory of Jody Taylor.

The Jody Taylor bigleaf maple is not identified with a plaque. Probably he would have wanted it that way. But when I first saw it in January 2018, it was sporting a fun-filled decoration of a plump dancer. I wondered who had hung that ornament.

The Jody Taylor Memorial Tree is planted southwest of Stanley Park Brewing's new Restaurant & Brewpub. That building has been through several iterations. It was built in 1930 as a sports pavilion (that is its name on the maps on pages 154 and 156) for golfers and tennis players, nestled between the two sporting areas. After being renamed several times, the building became the Fish House in 1991, a name it held until 2015, when the restaurant owners decided not to renew their lease and the Park Board started looking for new tenants.

In front of the former sports pavilion is a very bushy Harry Lauder's walking stick (*Corylus avellana* 'Contorta'). This uncommon hazel cultivar has found a number of homes in Stanley Park and seems to grow slowly but well.

Going across the putting green, I have to make note of two special trees across Stanley Park Drive in the median beside the Second Beach parking lot: a Norway maple (*Acer platanoides* 'Crimson King') that is a gorgeous rich brown, and a Japanese pagoda tree (*Sophora japonica*), with its sprays of pinnately compound leaves, also known as a scholar tree. (*Pinnate* means resembling a feather.) This tree is seldom noticed by anyone—let alone studied under—because park visitors are instead figuring out how to use the parking lot machine directly beside it.

Back on the putting green, there are three trees to note especially: a variegated sycamore maple (*Acer pseudoplatanus* 'Leopoldii'), whose leaves display various shades of green and lime green; the scarlet oak (*Quercus coccinea*), with its deeply grooved leaves and red fall colours; and the Hungarian oak (*Quercus frainetto* 'Forest Green'), well named for its shiny dark green foliage.

Next to the northwest-to-southeast path that bisects the green is an enormous bigleaf maple that towers over the crosswalk across Stanley Park Drive. I have seen wedding couples stand below it for their official photographs. In the fall, the tree's dinner-plate-sized yellow leaves make an ochre carpet for yards around, until the park gardeners sweep them up for composting.

Walking between a Norway spruce (*Picea abies*) and a western redcedar (*Thuja plicata*), you will find an English oak in the north corner of the putting green. Below it you will see a plaque that intrigued me when I first spotted it. (Actually, this was the first tree plaque I had seen anywhere in the park. Afterwards, I started looking for them.)

Queen Elizabeth Oak
(from the Royal Forest at Windsor)
Planted on Coronation Day
May 12th 1937

Fall colour of variegated sycamore maple (*Acer pseudoplatanus* 'Leopoldii').

Once I saw the words *Coronation Day* and *Queen Elizabeth*, I was expecting the date to be the coronation of Queen Elizabeth II. But this is the coronation date of George VI and Elizabeth Bowes-Lyon, crowned king and queen of the United Kingdom and the Dominions of the British Commonwealth, at a time when Canada was still a dominion. They had visited Vancouver in 1901 during their cross-Canada tour, in their capacities as the Duke and Duchess of Cornwall and York, and received a festive welcome.

May 12, 1937, was the date originally set for the coronation of King Edward VIII (he visited Stanley Park as the Prince of Wales in 1919). When he abdicated his throne in favour of marrying divorcee Wallis Simpson, the coronation date instead became the one for King George VI and Queen Elizabeth.

The tree was 10 feet tall when Alice Ashworth Townley, former park commissioner, planted it on that rainy day in 1937.[4] Townley was the first female Park Board commissioner. She served from 1928 to 1935.[5]

This particular specimen of English oak (*Quercus robur*), which began its life as an acorn in Windsor Great Park, England, has not yet reached its full height and spread here in Vancouver, even now, eighty-three years later. I feel it is suffering from crown shyness (see chapter 8), growing in the shade of the much bigger western redcedar to the south (25 on the map). An alternative theory is that it is not well, a theory I will raise once more in chapter 33.

English oak planted for Queen Elizabeth on the occasion of the coronation of George VI and Elizabeth Bowes-Lyon as king and queen of the United Kingdom in 1937.

CLOCKWISE FROM LEFT

Four California giants on the putting green: left to right, giant sequoia (*Sequoiadendron giganteum*), coast redwood (*Sequoia sempervirens*), incense cedar (*Calocedrus decurrens*), and another giant sequoia.

Immature seed cones on a giant sequoia.

Fronds of sharp, overlapping scaly leaves of a giant sequoia (*Sequoiadendron giganteum*) hang in front of tree trunk.

▶ OPPOSITE The avenue of mostly horse chestnut trees leads from the sports pavilion to English Bay.

I wonder whether King George VI and Queen Elizabeth visited that tree when they were driven through Stanley Park as part of their cross-Canada tour in 1939, mid-May to mid-June. I very much doubt it.

To the east of the English oak are the California forest giants (32 to 35) found on many maps of the big trees of Vancouver. If you walk among these gentle sentinels, you will learn the true meaning of the word *awe* for

yourself. Each one seems to beggar description, and each one is beautiful in its own right. For instance, the trunk of the incense cedar (*Calocedrus decurrens*) splits into two before the foliage begins, and yet the tree still maintains the tall oval shape for which it is known.

The two giant sequoias are stunning.

And pretty soon we are back at the old sports pavilion. An avenue of horse chestnut trees was planted, probably around 1930, in a straight line directly south from the pavilion toward Beach Avenue and English Bay. The easterly row of trees in this avenue creates the westerly edge of a triangle of horse chestnut trees. On this triangular lawn behind Stanley Park Lawn Bowling Club, people play Frisbee, toss balls, run their dogs, have picnics, and avoid the ubiquitous goose droppings.

The trees in this area are predominantly white horse chestnuts (*Aesculus hippocastanum*). One tree in the avenue, though, is a very rare tree, a shagbark hickory (*Carya ovata*) (45 on the map). A native of eastern North America, this mature tree fits in very well with the horse chestnuts, with its compound leaves and similar height and crown shape. Its bark, however, is definitely shaggier; its flowers are quite different, growing singly rather than in racemes; and from a distance, the foliage is a far deeper green. I suspect this was another of the trees planted to supply edible nuts for the eastern grey squirrels purchased from New York.

The Stanley Park heronry begins in a couple of trees that grow east of the tennis courts and north of the Vancouver Park Board offices. Herons have been building their nests on this peninsula for eons; photos from a century ago show a different location.

As Stanley Park Ecology Society explains, "Stanley Park is home to one of the largest urban great blue heron (*Ardea herodias fannini*) colonies in North America. They have been nesting at their current location behind 2099 Beach Avenue since 2001."[6] The nest trees are entirely deciduous: horse chestnuts (as in the photo at the beginning of this chapter), some maples, four English oaks planted many years ago, and a few London plane trees. Herons probably favour deciduous trees because their abundant summer foliage protects the eggs and fledglings from predation by the bald eagles that live in the park.

The Park Board has set up a high-definition webcam to show activity in heron nests from March (courtship and nest building) through July (egg laying, hatching, parenting, and fledgling flight).[7]

There is one more tree to note. It is the red oak (*Quercus rubra*) at the corner of Park Lane and Beach Avenue, near the Vancouver Park Board offices. A gorgeous specimen,

TOP The bark of a giant sequoia (*Sequoiadendron giganteum*) shows damage from climbing grey squirrels.

BOTTOM Snow settles around the Vancouver Park Board offices. The red oak is now bereft of leaves.

with vertically ridged bark and five- to seven-lobed leaves that are three-pronged, bristle-tipped, and stretching out like fingers, this tree provides shade to all who pass under its great spread. In every season, I feel it beckoning me into the history of Stanley Park's trees.

12.

24

Trees on the Promenade

The birds used to fly over in the evening at what is now Lost Lagoon,
and the interesting part is that if you go to the magnificent Causeway
which has replaced the old wooden bridge, you can see the same night
flight of wild ducks despite all the civilisation.

William August Roedde of G.A. Roedde Bookbinders,
in conversation with Major Matthews, August 3, 1943

THE TREED WALKING area on the causeway—both the flat area and the slope—used to be called the Promenade. Let's reinstate that name.

By 1925, the Promenade was close to being finished (the first time). Excavation had begun nine years earlier, and it would take one more year to complete the causeway. Trees had been planted. On the opposite page is an image of the causeway in 1931. On the right are deciduous trees; on the left I can see at least one conifer growing between the deciduous trees. The median contains flower beds.

The next good photographs of these Promenade trees were taken on January 28, 1936. The Promenade was part of the route to the memorial at Malkin Bowl for King George V, an event that drew thousands of British Columbians to the park. The Promenade trees had grown, and there were by then some tall deciduous trees growing in the flower beds in the median.

A swath was cut through the park in 1937, making room for a road to connect Vancouver with the North Shore via the Lions Gate Bridge—a perilous undertaking. A YouTube video with footage from 1938 shows the Lions Gate Bridge almost finished.[1] What incredible dexterity and

◄ OPPOSITE The causeway looking north in 1931. Young trees are growing on the Promenade.

TOP Vancouverites gather on the Promenade for the memorial for King George V in 1936.

BOTTOM The approach to Stanley Park and to Lion's Gate Bridge are now one and the same. Both subways are visible in this photo.

bravery those builders displayed, running up and down that bridge during its construction. Acres of park forest were cleared for this three-lane thoroughfare.

Recognizing that traffic would now increase at the Georgia Street entrance to the park, the city built two subways under the causeway. One is at the bottom of the Chilco Street slope; in 2018 it was overhung with Oregon grape (*Berberis aquifolium*) and enticing, sweet-smelling purple butterfly bush (*Buddleja*). The other subway connected Lost Lagoon with Rose Cottage, where administrative staff worked, and the plant nursery, where gardeners worked. You can see how much bigger the Promenade trees had grown.

Let us look at the trees one by one on the flat part of the Promenade, starting nearest the Georgia Street entrance. The trees in the Promenade area have changed over the years. Below is a chart to show the ones growing there now. The first trees I see are a pair of welcoming Norway maples (*Acer platanoides*; 2 and 3 on the map) that turn a glorious sunny yellow in the fall.

The tree nearest the seawall's 0 miles/ km sign (latitude 49.2952 N | longitude 123.13583 W) is a copper beech (*Fagus sylvatica purpurea*; 1 on the map). Its bark is light grey, smooth yet wrinkled, like a mama elephant's legs. It's the kind of trunk lovers write their initials in and surround with hearts. It feels generous. In spring, its small brown female flowerets signify that

CLOCKWISE FROM THE TOP
The welcoming Norway maple turns yellow in the fall. The copper beech and the deodar cedar provide contrast.

The subway for bikes and pedestrians to pass safely under Highway 99 is overhung in April 2018 with blossoming Oregon grape (*Berberis aquifolium*).

Oregon grape grows over the subway from the West End to Stanley Park's Promenade in July.

Trees on the Promenade

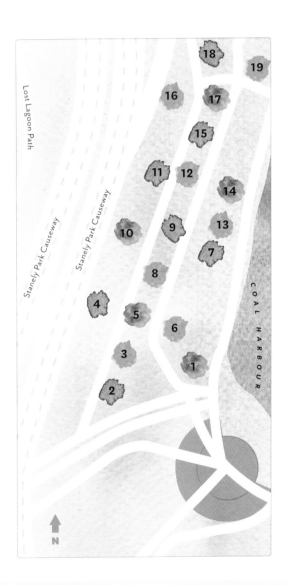

1. Copper beech (*Fagus sylvatica purpurea*)
2. Norway maple (*Acer platanoides*)
3. Norway maple (*Acer platanoides*)
4. Himalayan cedar (*Cedrus deodara*), a.k.a. deodar cedar
5. Box elder (*Acer negundo*), a.k.a. Manitoba maple
6. Himalayan cedar (*Cedrus deodara*), a.k.a. deodar cedar
7. Northern catalpa (*Catalpa speciosa*)
8. Norway maple (*Acer platanoides*)
9. Norway maple (*Acer platanoides*)
10. Northern catalpa (*Catalpa speciosa*)
11. Western redcedar (*Thuja plicata*)
12. Box elder (*Acer negundo*), a.k.a. Manitoba maple
13. Himalayan cedar windfall from 2006 windstorm
14. Himalayan cedar (*Cedrus deodara*), a.k.a. deodar cedar
15. Norway maple (*Acer platanoides*)
16. Manna ash (*Fraxinus ornus*), a.k.a. flowering ash
17. Norway maple (*Acer platanoides*)
18. Portuguese laurel (*Prunus lusitanica*)
19. Portuguese laurel (*Prunus lusitanica*)

it's a wind-pollinated tree; the male flowers are long-stemmed catkins. The tree's knees (its roots) are visible, bulging above the surrounding lawn. It has a beautifully bushy crown, like a fountain. Today in fall, the remains of last year's female beechnuts are on the grass, half eaten.

To the east of the Promenade is the Vancouver Rowing Club clubhouse, which has been in that location since it was towed into position in June 1905 from its previous location at the foot of Bute Street.

The two northern catalpas (*Catalpa speciosa*) on the Promenade (7 and 10 on the map) and the enormous one in the contiguous area of Devonian Park to the south are mature trees, probably reaching their hundredth birthday. Originally from the southeastern US, catalpas sport long black bean pods in winter and dark, bare, spreading branches in spring. Here in Canada, their seasonal patterns are delayed: not until late spring and early summer do the vast umbrella-like canopies start sprouting leaves, and in summer, gorgeous one-stemmed florescences.

CLOCKWISE FROM TOP LEFT
Leaves on copper beech emerge in late April.

English hawthorn (*Crataegus laevigata*) blossoms in mid-April.

The Vancouver Rowing Club.

Flower buds form on
the catalpas.

New spring growth
on deodar cedar
(*Cedrus deodara*).

This victim of the
windstorm of 2006
has provided many tree-
climbing opportunities
for youngsters of all ages.

The three Himalayan cedars (*Cedrus deodara*) on the Promenade are gorgeous (4, 6, and 14 on the map). Their common name is Himalayan cedar because they originated in the Western Himalayas. Another common name is deodar cedar. You might think this tree's common name *deodar* should be capitalized if you notice that it sounds like Diyodar, a city in west India. But that city is over a thousand kilometres from Western Himalaya. It turns out that *deodar* is close to a Sanskrit word, *devadāru*, meaning "wood of the gods" and so the epithet name can be lowercased. Presenting a range of greens—a light, bright green in the current year's young needles and a deeper green in older needles— deodars resemble graceful old dames in their crinolines. They hold their cones upright on their branches, like so many plump candles. Here on the wet west coast of BC, deodars have moss growing on their trunks.

On the Coal Harbour side of the Promenade, between a northern catalpa and a deodar cedar, is an erratically branched, debarked northern catalpa that was so heavily damaged by the windstorm of 2006 that it was deemed better to let it lie. It is 13 on the map. Nowadays, it is one of the most photographed trees around. Children and adults

TOP Box elders, a.k.a. Manitoba maples (*Acer negundo*), are in blossom.

BOTTOM The sun rises in the east, behind the city, the Rowing Club, and another tulip tree.

alike love climbing its buttressed roots and sitting on its sturdy limbs.

The box elders are perhaps better known as Manitoba maples (*Acer negundo*), a maple native to Canada (5 and 12). It is an atypical maple that bears pinnately compound leaves, long clusters of male flowers, and equally long ribbons of cream-coloured female flowers—no samaras and no palm-shaped, five-fingered leaves.

A manna ash (*Fraxinus ornus*) is the last tree you'll see on the flat Promenade area. May is the best month to see this ash's white panicles of flowers.

Take a seat for a moment on one of the many park benches under a Promenade tree. Facing west, you can watch vehicular traffic hurrying to its destination. Facing east, you will see the Vancouver Rowing Club, its busy docks, and its many patrons. Float planes buzz overhead en route between Vancouver Island and Coal Harbour. If you like people watching, you're in luck: the foot and bicycle traffic through the Promenade is constant—children in strollers, people on rollerblades, adults walking their dogs, groups of teenagers visiting from local schools.

Setting off again, the oldest trees beside the sloping ramp were planted earlier than the trees in the flat part of the Promenade, sometime in the early 1920s. The Lord Stanley statue wasn't erected for another forty years (see chapter 28).

At the bottom of the ramp are two Portuguese laurels (*Prunus lusitanica*), a species that the Stanley Park Ecology Society (SPES) now lists as an emergent species in its guide to invasive plant management.[2] In other words, SPES considers Portuguese laurel a problem. These two have grown so large, they create an archway that every cyclist, rollerblader, dog walker, adult, and child goes under when they use this park entrance. And in the fall, the treads on people's shoes or tires, or their dogs' paws, will pick up some of the laurels' dark purple berries (*drupes*) and spread the species around the park.

Nevertheless, these are handsome, bushy trees.

Halfway along the wall to the west is a mature saucer magnolia (*Magnolia × soulangeana*). This hybrid is named for its showy, pink, early spring flowers. Farther along, under the ramp (where the slope used to go down but now continues to climb up over Stanley Park Drive), are two young witch hazel plants (*Hamamelis virginiana*) that I find very appealing. The larger plant has become the size of a tree, and its unmistakable wispy late winter flowers are a deep coral-red. The younger bush beside it grows flowers that are the more typical yellow. This genus is unusual because it's one of the few trees in North America whose branches carry flowers, ripe fruit, and leaf buds at the same time. The first time I smelled witch

Witch hazel leaves lose their green colour and deepen through fall with coral and peach tones into blush red in October.

hazel growing, I was absolutely charmed by its fragrance.

Looking to the trees beside the wall on the east slope, you will see a Lawson cypress (*Chamaecyparis lawsoniana*), with its tiny octagonal blue seeds; an English hawthorn (*Crataegus laevigata*) with its three-lobed leaves and profusion of white spring flowers; a southern catalpa (*Catalpa bignonioides*) that flowers later than its cousin, the northern catalpa; and an ash, perhaps a narrow-leaf ash (*Fraxinus angustifolia*).

Let the constancy of this almost century-old planting calm your day as you watch the comings and goings all around.

25

Salmon Stream Valley

*Stanley Park is home to several bald eagle nests, with four to five active
in a given year. The Stanley Park Ecology Society (SPES) has monitored
active nests in the Park since 2004, with surveys conducted every year …
The SPES team observes how many breeding pairs have returned to the
Park and how many eaglets are successfully reared from each nest.*

"Eagles Nesting in Stanley Park," Stanley Park Ecology Society website

"SALMON STREAM VALLEY" is my name for a rectangular area of
the park that is between the Rock Garden, Stanley Park Pavilion,
the Theatre Under the Stars box office, and Malkin Bowl in the
west; the Vancouver Aquarium and Avison Way in the east; the
number 19 bus loop and the Stanley Park Railway in the north;
and the Information Booth parking lot, the Horse-Drawn Tours
sales kiosk, and Coal Harbour in the south (latitude from 49.298
to 49.300 N | longitude from 123.1321 to 123.1328 W). Find 25 in the
map in the introduction.

Looking at that 1911 map, it's clear that in this location there were
originally three connecting ponds and a waterway that led to a seal
pond.[1] Nowadays, Salmon Stream is an artificial salmon stream that
flows from the aquarium to Coal Harbour. BC Hydro spearheaded
the salmon stream project in the year 2000, moving the focus from
the vacated zoo to salmon.

But enough about animals. Let's return to the trees. There are
quite a few interesting individual trees and several groves of tree
species in this area.

◀ OPPOSITE Star-shaped
leaves of sweetgum
(*Liquidambar styraciflua*)
turn gorgeous reds and
burgundies in fall.

In the fall, the Information Booth parking lot is ablaze with the gorgeous yellow-to-orange colours of a grove of sweetgums (*Liquidambar styraciflua*), the colours making the trees look like a grove of maples. The way to know that a sweetgum is not a variety of maple is not perhaps by its five sharply lobed, star-shaped palmate leaves but by its round and very prickly, spiny seed pods. In this case, I wish the Park Board had found a sweetgum cultivar that dropped fewer hazards to small paws and young knees, despite the gorgeous fall colouring.

Leaving the parking lot behind and walking north, you'll see the first of the Painters' Circles. Japanese stuartias (*Stewartia pseudocamellia*) surround the west of the circle. The two spellings of this beautiful ornamental, *Stewartia* and *stuartia*, owe their origin to Carl Linnaeus's misspelling of the Scottish family name Stuart. The eighteenth-century Swedish botanist Linnaeus was instrumental in formalizing binomial nomenclature of the species of all living things. His misspellings will live on.

Farther west of the next Painters' Circle is a gorgeous stand of dawn redwoods (*Metasequoia glyptostroboides*). These are glorious in every season, with their braided trunks, acute-angled branches, fronds of feathery green foliage in spring, delicate buff-coloured foliage in fall, and winter skeletons. Of the three species of redwood trees, this is the only one considered deciduous.

CLOCKWISE FROM
TOP LEFT
An opportunistic
deciduous tree grows
in a deadhead.

The blossom of a
Japanese stuartia
(*Stewartia pseudocamellia*)
does indeed look a bit
like a camellia, leading
to its Latin name.

A wild rose has found a
sunny spot to grow its
edible hips.

A photogenic dawn
redwood.

Sweet chestnut
(*Castanea sativa*) in July.

There are several youngsters in this gathering that are very photogenic.

Encircled within this stand is a bigleaf maple stump—an early park giant—that's not willing to give up life yet. The term "strange bedfellows" comes to mind as I look at this relic of a tree stump, with a sword fern growing out of it on one side and a very young, tall, hopeful *Metasequoia* growing on the other.

Going farther west, you'll find several trees planted specifically to provide food for the grey squirrels after they were released in the park in 1914. They include English oaks (*Quercus robur*), with their abundant acorns; one or more mulberries (*Morus*), with their long, blackberry-like fruit (I haven't found

these yet); some European hornbeams (*Carpinus betulus*), with their clusters of winged seeds (I have yet to find these too); and a sweet chestnut (*Castanea sativa*), with its sharp-toothed oval leaves and its edible (even for humans) nuts.

One very tall sweet chestnut reaches for the sky at latitude 49.2984 N | longitude 123.13256 W, and a young one is developing opposite the memorial to Queen Victoria on the seawall side of Park Road. Another is growing directly east of the Stanley Park Pavilion at latitude 49.2998 N | longitude 123.13279 W. And another growing west of Brockton Oval was heavy with fruit in August 2019. These are among the tallest sweet chestnuts in North America, ever since a sweet chestnut blight (fungus *Cryphonectria parasitica*) devastated American chestnuts throughout the eastern part of the continent. The American Chestnut Foundation is committed to "restoring the American chestnut tree to our eastern woodlands to benefit our environment, our wildlife, and our society."[2] They are accomplishing this through back-breeding to a blight-resistant species and reforestation.

Here, a solemn assembly of western redcedars invites you inside its sacred space to breathe in the quiet air and its long-remembered times. Standing inside, accepting this invitation, I am reminded of a multitude of reasons why people tell me "I *love* trees." Somehow, trees bring us home to ourselves. My friend Kaye Kerlande Siouras tells me, "Trees help me to connect with the moon, with my inner self. Trees help me believe in myself, give me strength and vision. The manifestation of the love a tree possesses is grand. The way a tree speaks is pure and gentle."

Returning to the Painters' Circle (latitude 49.2987 N | longitude 123.1319 W) and travelling north and northwest, you'll find many interesting individual trees. First is a giant Douglas-fir (latitude 49.299 N | longitude 123.13277 W), the tallest around, according to the bald eagles that nest here year after year (mentioned in chapter 10, "Trail Trees"). Though it can be a bit dangerous to walk under an aerie when it's being built or repaired—because of an eagle's haphazard way of building its nest—it's intriguing to walk around under such a tree and see what's been on the menu during the past week. Bits of wings, a variety of feathers, slender bones, and small skulls adorned the ground the last time I walked by. Fish from as far south as the mouth of the Fraser River would have been on the menu too, but every scrap of salmon was consumed. There's a clear sightline to this aerie from a path south of the Stanley Park Pavilion.[3]

Near a paved path is a tall Douglas-fir that a group of Junior Forest Wardens planted in 1936 in memory of a chief forester. The plaque reads,

This tree planted May 8, 1936, by the Junior Forest Wardens of British Columbia in memory of P.Z. Caverhill, Chief Forester of British Columbia, 1920–35.

Two Canada geese are caring for an unusually large gaggle of twenty-five goslings.

From New Brunswick, Caverhill was the third-ever chief forester for the provincial government. During his tenure, early nurseries and experimental forests were established and inventory improvements were made. His long service in survival mode during much of the Depression was very taxing. He died in office in 1935.

Not only is Caverhill remembered through the tree planted by the Junior Forest Wardens, but when the BC Forest Service (it has changed its name multiple times before and since) purchased the *Yurinohana*, a

This Douglas-fir is twice plaqued.

22-metre-long freighter, for use as a patrol vessel, she became the *P.Z. Caverhill*. The freighter retained that name until new owners renamed her again in 1951.[4]

In the lawn just north of the Caverhill tree is another Junior Forest Warden Douglas-fir with a plaque describing not just one but two dedication ceremonies.

THE JUNIOR FOREST WARDENS TREE

This tree was planted on May 2, 1931, by the Honourable N. S. Lougheed, Minister of Lands for British Columbia in Earth gathered from all parts of this province, in honour of the Junior Forest Wardens of the Canadian Forestry Association.
"God has lent us the Earth for our life. It is a great entail. It belongs as much to those who come after us as to us."—RUSKIN

Rededicated September 18, 1988 unveiled by the Honourable Gerald Merrithew, Minister of State (Forestry). Plaque contributed by the Truck Loggers Association.

It too grows tall and straight.

The Junior Forest Warden program began in 1929 in response to the formation by a group of boys of an outdoor club to assist their local Canadian Forestry Association officers. An entry in the Vancouver Park Board minutes from May 1947 refers to the service the Junior Forest Wardens were providing to patrol Stanley Park "for fires and molesters."[5] This

Some monarch trees grow in the Salmon Stream Valley.

was the first environmental youth movement in BC, and it continues to provide outdoor fitness training for young people.

Down a path and around a corner at the back of the Rock Garden is a plaqued tree, a bushy white camellia, commemorating American suffragist Frances Elizabeth Willard.[6]

Commemorating the Centennial of Francis E. Willard
Planted Sept. 28th 1939—
by the Woman's Christian Temperance
Union of Vancouver District

Frances Willard participated in the founding of the Women's Christian Temperance Union and became its second president in 1879.[7] On a visit to Victoria, BC, in July 1883, Willard helped Canadian suffragists form a BC provincial union. However, not until April 1917, thirty-four years later, did BC women actually gain the vote.

Mrs. James Esselmont planted the white camellia in Stanley Park on the centenary of Willard's birth, in front of "one of the largest gatherings of city women of that decade."[8] That planting ceremony was observed by Paul R. Josselyn, the American consul general in Vancouver at the time.

Several leafy paths leading east take walkers to a concrete structure that is the old polar bear den. At one time, four bears lived in this "grotto"—Nootka, Jubilee II,

LEFT The tall western redcedar that grows at the Vancouver Aquarium is growing candelabra branches.

RIGHT A long, hot summer in 2018 deepened the range of reds and russets on the deciduous trees at the old polar bear den.

Prince Rupert, and Princess Rupert. Born on Southampton Island in Hudson Bay, they were donated to the Stanley Park Zoo by the Hudson's Bay Company.[9] Tuk was the fifth and last bear to live in this den. For me, the charm of this space nowadays is provided by the gorgeous overhanging ornamental maples that are so colourful in the fall, as colourful as the park's history.

One last tree needs to be singled out for recognition in this Salmon Stream Valley. It is the tall, lone western redcedar that grows at the Vancouver Aquarium, an evergreen so tall that I had to stand back a long way to see how it has broken off and split at the top in what seemed to me like quite strange ways until I learned that this candelabra branching is typical for western redcedars.

26

Totem Poles Were Once Trees

Before a cedar tree is harvested for a totem pole, many coastal First Nations communities will perform a ceremony of gratitude and respect in honour of the tree. Several trees may be inspected before a particular tree is chosen for its beauty and character.

Indigenous Foundations, First Nations Studies Program website, University of British Columbia

TOTEM POLES ARE "one of the most recognizable cultural symbols of the Pacific Northwest."[1] Yet I do not necessarily understand them. For me—a non-Indigenous person—totem poles are difficult to understand.

From reading about the subject, I understand that a totem pole gathers to itself visual reminders of the humans, animals, and spirits important to its people. A totem pole also states that the place it was carved to occupy is its people's land, making it as much a statement of belonging as an art form. In choosing a suitable tree to carve into a totem, Pacific Northwest carvers pay respect and offer gratitude to the chosen tree. This is what encouraged me to include a few words about totem poles in this book on the legacy trees of Stanley Park.

Some Coast Salish totem poles and carvings have occupied places here and there in Stanley Park. There is currently one in the Stanley Park Train Plaza, though it was carved and erected purposefully for that location in 1991, and a couple more along the railway route itself. After settlers moved to Western Canada in the nineteenth century, bringing with them new carving implements and different

A totem pole at
Lumberman's Arch
in 1946.

cultural and design values, totem poles
became what a westerner's eye might consider more decorative and artistic.[2]

In 1912 an area east of Brockton Oval
was set aside for an "Indian village," and
two totem poles and two Thunderbird
house posts were donated to the park.[3]
This is what set the precedent for the

location—nothing to do with Coast Salish
traditions.

The successful eviction trials of 1925
allowed the city to remove all inhabitants from the park, including those of
Indigenous heritage (see chapter 13).
Having won its court case, the city did not
hurry to carry out the evictions, but by the

1930s, most park dwellers had gone. Only Tim Cummings, a resolute man born near the shore at Brockton Point, remained in the park in his own home.

In 1936, the City of Vancouver celebrated its golden jubilee, and as part of those celebrations, it brought in more totem poles to add to the ones at Brockton Point. Four were Kwakiutl poles from Vancouver Island, one was from the Tlingit Nation in Kingcome Inlet, farther up the BC coast, and one was from Haida Gwaii (then called the Queen Charlotte Islands).[4] All but one of the totem poles were carved in places up and down the Northwest Coast, not in the Lower Mainland. This is what pushes the Brockton Point poles outside their context: they have been removed from their place of meaning and brought here. The space is a totem pole museum.

Also for the golden jubilee celebrations, Chief Joe Capilano of North Vancouver—Pauline Johnson's old *tillicum* ("friend" in Chinook jargon)—carved the Thunderbird Dynasty Pole, which commemorated the meeting of the Squamish people and Captain George Vancouver on June 12, 1792.[5] Qoitchetahl, also known as Andrew Paul, delivered an address at the grand jubilee ceremony held at Prospect Point on August 25, 1936.

For a while, the Thunderbird Pole stayed at Prospect Point. In the 1940s, there were several totem poles at Lumberman's Arch, overlooking the beach in much the same way

Totems at Brockton Point.

the original Coast Salish meeting houses had done before.

Then in 1962, most of the totem poles were gathered up and brought to what is now called the Totem Pole Interpretive Centre at Brockton Point. Despite the fact that the Brockton Point poles are Vancouver's most visited tourist attraction,[6] most of the nine come from Indigenous communities in other parts of BC, because Coast Salish people have not been prolific totem pole carvers. (Interestingly, a Kwakiutl totem pole replaced the caduceus symbol on the City of Vancouver's coat of arms in 1969.)[7] These days, the poles at the Totem

The rounded crown of a sweetgum behind one of Susan Point's three welcoming gateways.

Pole Interpretive Centre at Brockton Point are replicas, the originals having become too weatherworn.

Fulfilling the desire to have art created by local Indigenous artists at Brockton Point, Musqueam artist Susan Point carved three welcoming gateways, and these were erected in the Totem Pole Interpretive Centre in 2007. Known collectively as *People Amongst the People*, these gateways are fittingly made of western redcedar. A charming sweetgum (*Liquidambar styraciflua*) grows south of Susan Point's southern welcoming gateway.

Now, in the twenty-first century, the City of Vancouver is going through a period of re-examining its history. In the interests of adhering to the recommendations of the Truth and Reconciliation Commission of Canada, the Park Board has employed a full-time archaeologist. The Stanley Park Intergovernmental Working Group is a unique forum for Park Board staff and members of the Musqueam, Squamish, and Tsleil-Waututh Nations to work together on a long-term comprehensive plan for Stanley Park, a plan that honours Indigenous heritage. Vancouver's Urban Indigenous Peoples' Advisory Committee is also consulted in park planning.

Many Vancouver institutions now recognize that we live, work, and play on the unceded territories of the Musqueam, Squamish, and Tsleil-Waututh Nations.

A European beech displays its full fall glory.

Some place names within BC have changed; for example, the Queen Charlotte Islands are now called Haida Gwaii and Siwash Rock is also being known by its Squamish name of Slahkayulsh. These are some of the accomplishments of the Canadian Truth and Reconciliation Commission that was mandated to redress wrongs and reconcile Canadians and Indigenous peoples.

A little to the southeast of the totem poles stands Luke Marston's *Shore to Shore* bronze sculpture of his great-great-grandparents: Portuguese Joe Silvey and Kwatleemaat (Lucy), a Sechelt matriarch. Portuguese Joe's first wife, Khaltinaht, a noblewoman from the Musqueam and Squamish Nations, completes the circle. The ceremonial installation of this sculpture drew a big crowd in 2015.

When you leave the Totem Pole Interpretive Centre, go west, through the expansive border of evergreen and deciduous trees. A Pacific madrone (*Arbutus menziesii*) shares root space with a western redcedar. The gorgeous spreading crown of a European beech (*Fagus sylvatica*) provides shade and cool from heat in the summer, brilliant amber and golden and russet leaf colour in the fall, and beautiful architecture in the winter. A mature sweetgum (*Liquidambar styraciflua*) with very few prickly fruits—a different cultivar from those planted at the Information Booth—is well worth searching out. It is near the north part of the seawall, behind the interpretive centre. This sweetgum is as well established as the sweetgum near mile zero on the seawall; perhaps they were planted at the same time.

27

Shakespeare Garden Trees

And Adam was a gardener.

Henry VI, Part II, IV, ii, 136

THE VANCOUVER SHAKESPEARE Society was going strong in 1932 when they joined forces with the Kilbe Shakespeare Circle. Together, they planned to do something special for both Shakespeare and Vancouver in 1936, the year of the city's golden jubilee.[1] The Shakespeareans decided it was time to celebrate the Bard of Avon, not with just another tree but with an entire arboretum.

An invitation arrived on the desk of the Governor General of the day, Lord Tweedsmuir, to travel to Vancouver and officially open the Shakespeare Garden.

Actually, he and Lady Tweedsmuir had a very busy time in late August 1936, opening the Seaforth Armoury, touring City Hall, inspecting boy scouts and wolf cubs on Ceperley Playground, visiting the City of Vancouver Archives and meeting Major James Matthews, and laying a wreath at the cenotaph. And more.

Tweedsmuir had literary leanings himself, though nothing like Shakespeare's. His pen name was John Buchan, and he was the author of *The Thirty-Nine Steps*, a "dime novel" he wrote at the beginning of the First World War when he was convalescing from a duodenal ulcer. Tweedsmuir described his "shocker" (the term used in England for a dime novel) as a "romance where the incidents defy the probabilities, and march just inside the borders of the possible."[2]

A plaque is affixed to the exterior of one of the works yard buildings abutting the Shakespeare Garden in the north (latitude 49.2996 N | longitude 123.1368 W).

SHAKESPEARE GARDEN

Developed to reflect the aspirations of early Vancouver, the Shakespeare Garden is a secluded arboretum of trees mentioned in the Bard's plays and poems.
The first tree was planted by Mrs. Jonathan Rogers in 1916 on the three hundred year anniversary of the Bard's death. Architect J.F. Watson designed and sculpted the Shakespeare monument in time for the garden's official opening in 1936 by the Governor General, Lord Tweedsmuir.

SPONSORED BY BRUCE MCINTYRE WATSON

Monument to William Shakespeare.

The Thirty-Nine Steps was made into a movie by Alfred Hitchcock.

I could find no photographic record of Lord and Lady Tweedsmuir's visit to Stanley Park, but his words at the unveiling were recorded:

> I like to think of Shakespeare as someone who lived and worked with flowers. He made his gardens beautiful and you have followed his pattern in true spirit. Nothing has amazed me more than the beauty and luxuriousness of the gardens. Shakespeare, I am sure, would have loved to live here. I have great pleasure in opening and dedicating these gardens.

Made of limestone and brick, John Francis Watson's Shakespeare Monument looked good for the first couple of decades, but it's now looking a bit weather-beaten from all the rain we get in Vancouver—over a thousand millimetres (45.4 inches) annually—and few people know of its existence.

SHAKESPEARE

1564–1616
He was not of an age but for all time

All these years later, I find it difficult to know how many trees the arboretum comprised at that opening. Sometime after

1977, the Vancouver Board of Parks and Recreation produced a tabloid sheet identifying each tree then growing in the Shakespeare Garden.

The original inscriptions nailed into a handful of the trees are now so weathered as to be illegible. Fortunately, the Vancouver Park Board rededicated the Shakespeare Garden in 1996 and replaced the original inscriptions with small tin sheets that will be legible for some years to come. Shakespearean actor and founder of Vancouver's popular Bard on the Beach Christopher Gaze, OBC, MSM, recited some pithy Shakespearean couplets at that event.

ONE, on the right, is a simple map of the plaqued Shakespeare Garden trees, showing number one as the Shakespeare Monument.

TWO is a western redcedar (*Thuja plicata*). Its Shakespearean quotation is this:

> Marcus, we are but shrubs, no cedars we;
> No big-bon'd men, fram'd of the Cyclops' size.
> *Titus Andronicus* IV, iii, 45–46

THREE is a western hemlock (*Tsuga heterophylla*). The quotation is erroneous, as this witches' brew refers to poison-hemlock (*Conium maculatum*) rather than a non-poisonous western hemlock:

> Root of hemlock, digg'd i' the dark.
> *Macbeth* IV, i, 25

Shakespeare Garden Plaqued Trees

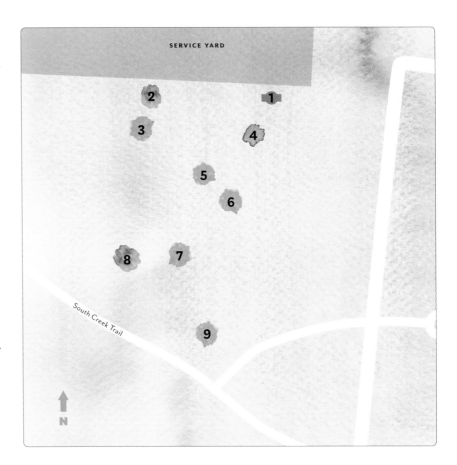

The leaves of the black locust seem to be lit from within.

FOUR is a red oak (*Quercus rubra*).

This particular red oak is a very tall specimen, though its spread is not very great, perhaps because of its many large neighbours. **FIVE** is a black locust (*Robinia pseudoacacia*).

The Shakespearean couplet refers to the locust that John the Baptist used to eat. Was that the swarming, migratory grasshopper, as approved for Jewish people in Leviticus 11:22—"Of these you may eat any kind of locust, katydid, cricket or grasshopper"? Those locusts are the ones associated with droughts and famines. But here in the Shakespearean couplet, *locust* instead refers to the tree, in true homonym style, though apparently the tree from which St. John ate was the carob tree (*Ceratonia siliqua*). The carob's pods and their contents are edible; the pods of a black locust tree are not. Both trees are in the pea family, Fabaceae.

Coloquintida, by the way, refers to the astringent fruit of the vine of Sodom. Enough said.

The word *black* refers to the bark of the black locust. The botanical term for locust's leaves is "pinnately compound," which means the leaflets grow on either side of the leaf stem, the way the barbs spread out on a bird's feather. The gentle lime-green colour of these compound leaves in sunshine seems to be lit from within, making the tree's wistful shape totally endearing. In later summer, the showy pendulous spring flowers become 10-centimetre-long seed pods (legumes) that endure well through rains and winter snows. This tree has outgrown the stage where it needed to grow thorns on its smaller branches to protect itself from herbivores.

SIX is a black walnut (*Juglans nigra*).

> Why, 'tis a cockle or a walnut-shell,
> A knack, a toy, a trick, a baby's cap.
> *The Taming of the Shrew* IV, iii, 67–68

Black here refers to the stain that walnuts emit when you try to get at the seed inside the shell—black enough that the shells were used to dye the homespun uniforms of Confederate soldiers during the American Civil War.[3] The pinnately compound leaves on a black walnut are similar to the leaves on a black locust tree, except that the black walnut has up to nineteen leaflets that are lanceolate (shaped like a lance) while the black locust leaf has up to nineteen oval leaflets about half the size. Of course, the different fruits (seed pods versus drupes),

the locust's thorns, and the great height of *Juglans* also make identification easier.

SEVEN is an Atlas cedar (*Cedrus atlantica*).

> And, like a mountain cedar, reach his branches
> To all the plains about him. Our children's children
> Shall see this, and bless Heaven.
> *Henry VIII* V, iv, 53–55

Once again, the tree and its couplet reference do not align. The common name "mountain cedar" actually refers to a juniper, *Juniperus ashei*, which is not a cedar at all and not even a close relative. Ah well. When these trees and couplets were wedded, the many tree apps and online search engines we have today had not yet been invented.

This Atlas cedar has grown into one of the giants in the Shakespeare Garden. An Atlas cedar bears short evergreen needles growing in clusters. Amazingly this is the same species (though a different cultivar) as the blue Atlas cedar the Vancouver Park Board has espaliered on the street side of its offices on Beach Avenue. There's another handsome specimen overhanging a bench halfway between the Lord Stanley and Robert Burns statues.

EIGHT is a comparatively young tree, not planted in 1936. I expect it was planted in the late 1970s. At the time when Vancouver Park Board's tabloid sheet identifying each tree in the Shakespeare Garden was produced, part

A grove of ten daybreak cherries (*Prunus × yedoensis*).

of this plaque had already broken away, so that it read as follows:

MEMORIAL PLAQUE

WYS THOMAS

Some years later, a new plaque was created:

This Oak commemorates Powys Thomas

1925–1977

Ah! "Powys" not "Wys." Powys is a Welsh name, one I recognize, the name of a Welsh county.

The tree is a red oak (*Quercus rubra*). So who was Powys Thomas? He was a Shakespearean actor who moved from Wales to Canada in 1956 to perform. Thomas first worked for the CBC and was one of the early performers at Ontario's Stratford Shakespeare Festival. He was instrumental in forming both the National Theatre School of Canada in 1960 and the Vancouver Playhouse Theatre Company in 1962.[4] Powys Thomas stayed in Vancouver long enough to perform in Vancouver Playhouse's production of *King Lear*. He returned to his native Wales in 1977 for a vacation and died suddenly while he was there. It is clear from the tree planted in his honour that he was much appreciated by audience members and actors alike.

NINE is a grove of ten daybreak cherries (*Prunus × yedoensis*). I hunted long and hard for the tenth plaque, without success; perhaps the tree that held it succumbed to disease. However, I found the quotation on Vancouver Park Board's's tabloid sheet.

> So we grew together,
> Like to a double cherry, seeming parted,
> But yet an union in partition;
> Two lovely berries moulded on one stem.
> *A Midsummer-Night's Dream* III, ii, 208–11

I write about this grove of cherry blossom trees in chapter 22, "Ornamental Cherry Trees."

At one time, a western white pine (*Pinus monticola*) planted with this group also carried a Shakespearean quotation:

> But when from under this terrestrial ball
> He fires the proud tops of the eastern pines.
> *King Richard II*, III, ii, 41–42

As happens sometimes when trees become diseased, that white pine (*western* rather than *eastern*) was cut down, its stump removed, and the lawn re-sown with grass seed. Now it is merely a memory. In late 2019, a magnolia with the cultivar name 'Butterflies' was moved in from elsewhere in the park to where the white pine used to be.

In the years following the unveiling of the Shakespeare memorial and the dedication of its trees by Governor General Lord Tweedsmuir in 1936, for the city's jubilee year, additional exotics and natives were planted in the grounds, making it a flourishing arboretum. (*Exotics* are trees that are not native to this part of BC.) Many of these ornamentals have the space to grow into superb specimens.

The Shakespeare Garden is one of my favourite places in the park. I walk here in every kind of weather. There is something so compelling about standing among these luxurious specimens, seeing life through their timeline, breathing in their serenity.

No doubt you will find a favourite tree among these beauties. I will introduce you to some of my favourites and then let you find your own from the map and the list below.

TOP LEFT It is cool under the umbrella canopy of the fernleaf beech.

TOP RIGHT The leaves of the fernleaf beech look different in every season.

More Shakespeare Garden Trees

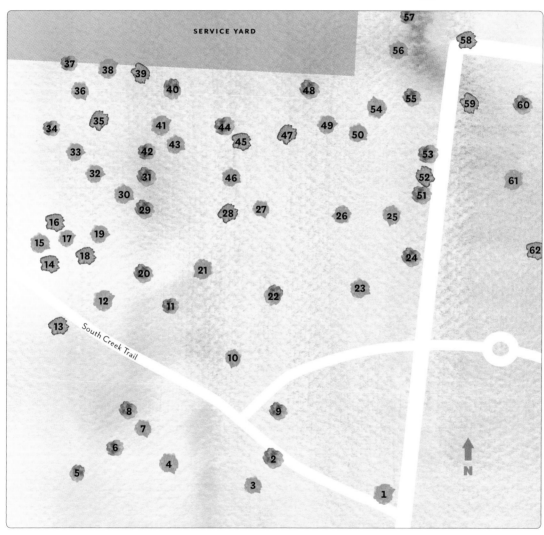

TO IDENTIFY THESE ornamental and native trees, I have used the tabloid sheet produced after 1977 by the Vancouver Board of Parks and Recreation, combined with the map created in 2006 by the Park Board's urban forester Bill Stephen for his chapter in *Wilderness on the Doorstep*.[5] My map includes the plaqued trees described on pages 195 to 199.

Flowering ash

1. Japanese snowbell (*Styrax japonicus*)

2. Gum tree (*Eucalyptus*)

3. Brazilian giant-rhubarb (*Gunnera manicata*), a.k.a. dinosaur food

4. Field maple (*Acer campestre*)

5. Snake bark maple (*Acer davidii* subsp. *davidii*)

6. Coast redwood (*Sequoia sempervirens*), a.k.a. California redwood

7. Lawson cypress (*Chamaecyparis lawsoniana*)

8. European hazelnut (*Corylus avellana*)

9. European hazelnut (*Corylus avellana* 'Purpurea')

10. Daybreak cherry (*Prunus × yedoensis*), plaqued

11. Lawson cypress (*Chamaecyparis lawsoniana*)

12. London plane tree (*Platanus × hispanica* 'Bloodgood')

13. Daybreak cherry (*Prunus × yedoensis*)

14. Daybreak cherry (*Prunus × yedoensis*)

15. Black tupelo (*Nyssa sylvatica*)

16. Western redcedar (*Thuja plicata*)

17. Douglas-fir (*Pseudotsuga menziesii*)

18. Big tooth maple (*Acer saccharum* subsp. *grandidentatum*)

19. Ruby red horse chestnut (*Aesculus × carnea* 'Briotii')

20. Red oak (*Quercus rubra*), plaqued

21. Atlas cedar (*Cedrus atlantica*), plaqued

22. Fernleaf beech (*Fagus sylvatica* 'Aspleniifolia')

23. Japanese stuartia (*Stewartia seudocamellia*)

24. Paperbark maple (*Acer griseum*)

25. Arie Peters manna ash (*Fraxinus ornus* 'Arie Peters')

26. Tree of heaven (*Ailanthus altissima*)

27. Black walnut (*Juglans nigra*), plaqued

28. Sawara false cypress (*Chamaecyparis pisifera* 'Filifera')

29. Dawn redwood (*Metasequoia glyptostroboides*)

30. Western redcedar (*Thuja plicata*)

31. Western redcedar (*Thuja plicata*)

32. Weeping black tupelo (*Nyssa sylvatica* 'Pendula')

33. European ash (*Fraxinus excelsior*)

34. Coast redwood (*Sequoia sempervirens*), a.k.a. California redwood

35. Austrian black pine (*Pinus nigra* subsp. *laricio*), a.k.a. Corsican pine

36. Weeping black tupelo (*Nyssa sylvatica* 'Pendula')

37. Kentucky coffeetree (*Gymnocladus dioicus*)

38. Pacific dogwood (*Cornus nuttallii* 'Goldspot')

39. European white birch (*Betula pendula*), a.k.a. silver birch

40. Western redcedar (*Thuja plicata*), plaqued

41. Western hemlock (*Tsuga heterophylla*), plaqued

42. European mountain ash (*Sorbus aucuparia*)

43. Vine maple (*Acer circinatum*)

44. Plumose Sawara false cypress (*Chamaecyparis pisifera* 'Plumosa')

45. Tulip tree (*Liriodendron tulipifera*), a.k.a. yellow poplar

46. Black locust (*Robinia pseudocacia*), plaqued

47. Red oak (*Quercus rubra*), plaqued

48. Shakespeare Monument

49. Yew—either Westfelton (*Taxus baccata* 'Dovastoniana') or Japanese (*T. cuspidata* 'Intermedia')

50. Saucer magnolia (*Magnolia × soulangeana*)

51. Colorado blue spruce (*Picea pungens* 'Glauca')

52. Mountain hemlock (*Tsuga mertensiana*)

53. Serbian spruce (*Picea omorika*)

54. Rohani beech (*Fagus sylvatica* 'Rohanii')

55. Katsura (*Cercidiphyllum japonicum*)

56. Umbrella pine (*Sciadopitys verticillata*)

57. Japanese pagoda tree (*Sophora japonica*), a.k.a. scholar tree

58. Weeping beech (*Fagus sylvatica* 'Pendula')

59. Harry Lauder's walking stick (*Corylus avellana* 'Contorta')

60. Turner's oak (*Quercus turneri*, a.k.a. *Q. ilex × Q. robur*)

61. Nootka cypress (*Cupressus nootkatensis*, a.k.a. *Chamaecyparis nootkatensis*), a.k.a. yellow cedar

62. Maidenhair tree (*Ginkgo biloba*)

Tulip tree (*Liriodendron tulipifera*)

European mountain ash (*Sorbus aucuparia*)

◄ OPPOSITE A tree of heaven (*Ailanthus altissima*) reaches for the sky in the Shakespeare Garden.

The fernleaf beech (*Fagus sylvatica* 'Aspleniifolia,' 22 on the map), named for its intricately cut, feathery leaves, is outstanding. It has reached a big spread, as wide as it is tall. This is not a tree to grow on a small city lot! Under its long, sweeping branches is a carpet of dry, brown duff—the decaying litter of leaves and small branches that have fallen over time. Inside this low canopy is a whole other world, quiet and tranquil.

The tree of heaven (*Ailanthus altissima*, 26) is fascinating, so lofty and yet so unappreciated because of its strong ability to grow from suckers more easily than from seed. Indeed, it is considered an invasive weed in some US states. The Shakespeare Garden specimen is very tall, reaching for heaven, true to its name. Its alternate, pinnately compound leaves wave gently whenever there's a breeze.

The Rohani beech (*Fagus sylvatica* 'Rohanii,' 54) is a beauty, with its deep burgundy-coloured leaves and low, idiomatic branches wafting near the ground. It has clearly been growing in this garden for a long time.

Over to the east, this side of Pipeline Road, is a gorgeous *Ginkgo biloba* tree (62), surrounded in 2018 by a bed of bright red annuals to set it off. Like the tree of heaven,

the ginkgo is a native of China that seems to flourish here in our temperate climate. It is a miracle that the *Ginkgo* genus survived from 270 million years ago—the only species surviving in its division (Ginkgophyta), class (Ginkgoopsida), order (Ginkgoales),

TOP The species *Ginkgo biloba* has been traced back in the fossil record 270 million years.

BOTTOM Winter catkins on a Harry Lauder's walking stick.

and family (Ginkgoaceae). It has proven to be a beautiful pest-free and storm-resistant addition to any landscaping, as long as it is given the space to spread its wings, though the female tree is seldom planted because the odour of its fruit is rank. What I particularly like about ginkgo is the way its leaves surround its branches, like sleeves made of small green fans. In autumn, the bright yellow leaves fall together within a few days of each other.

Let's wander up the path that's heading toward the weeping beech. On the right of the path is a mature Harry Lauder's walking stick (*Corylus avellana* 'Contorta,' 59). Usually a shrub, this is definitely a tree. Also known as a corkscrew hazel, for its crinkled leaves, this is an intriguing species no matter the season, even when it sports a screwy winter skeleton.

The Harry Lauder this hazel cultivar refers to was the knighted Scottish comedic song-and-dance man. Sir Harry wrote the following—in Scots—in his book, *A Minstrel in France*:[6]

> You've seen ma sticks? Weel, it's Tom always hands me the richt one just as I'm aboot to step on the stage. If he gied me the stick I use in "She's Ma Daisy" when I was aboot to sing "I Love a Lassie" I believe I'd have tae ha' the curtain rung doon upon me. But he never has. I can trust old Tom.

Evidently, Sir Harry had a variety of walking sticks, including the highly contorted one for whom this tree is named.

My absolutely favourite tree in the park is the weeping beech (*Fagus sylvatica* 'Pendula,' 58 on the map) that grows in front of Rose Cottage. It's north of the walking path between the Shakespeare arboretum and the Rose Garden (latitude 2997 N | longitude 123.1363 W), looking like a thousand hanging green wands. I write about it in the introduction. For me, this beech tops off the area's enchantment. Rose Cottage was built in 1914, which makes me think this beech was planted soon after, making it over a hundred years old.

One of the things I find amazing is how difficult it is to capture that beech's beauty in a photo. I am either too far away to appreciate its spread or too close to feel its scale. That's partly the nature of my challenges with photographing trees. When I am inside a tree's reach, its hanging branches surround me with timelessness and peace; I feel that eternity is now, caught up here forever. I find myself looking up at this beech's crown, following the lean of its main trunk, and marvelling at its hanging green bounty.

You have my secret—I love beech trees. They feel so generous and eternal. See if this beech's charm appeals to you, too. Stand under it and dream awhile.

There's just one more tree that must be experienced to be admired. It's 57 on the map

LEFT My favourite tree in the park is the weeping beech (*Fagus sylvatica* 'Pendula') that grows in front of Rose Cottage north of the Shakespeare Garden.

BELOW Overwintering flower buds on a rhododendron growing behind Rose Cottage.

above, just behind the Service Yard sign—a Japanese pagoda tree (*Sophora japonica*). I understand how one of the common names for such a tree could be "scholar tree." What more conducive place for being a scholar than sitting under the shade of this tree! But I have to wonder how a tree whose native home is China could end up being called a *Japanese* pagoda tree.

Find your own favourite.

PART III

The Park
Grows Up

28

Trees around
Lord Stanley's Statue

*Major Matthews, Vancouver archivist, discovered a letter in 1950 that
promised that a monument would be erected. The letter was dated 1889.
The statue was erected in 1960.*

Lord Stanley, Public Art Registry, City of Vancouver website

A MIXTURE OF native and planted shrubs and trees grows around British sculptor Sydney March's larger-than-life bronze statue of Lord Stanley at the Georgia Street entrance to the park. Many of the trees would be the same ones that grew around the original park ranger's house and the first zoo, now the site of Lord Stanley's statue.

This statue was not built until 1960, seventy-one years after the dedication ceremony. We have Major Matthews, Vancouver's first city archivist, to thank that this statue exists at all. Always wanting to order one more memorial and one more statue, Matthews came across a promise that a statue would be erected to commemorate Lord Stanley's role in giving his name to Vancouver's first park and later dedicating it.

Matthews found that unfulfilled promise in a neglected letter in 1950 and commissioned world-renowned sculptor Sydney March to create the statue. March was nearing the end of his career and had won huge fame with commissions for the British royal family and others. Sydney sometimes worked alone and sometimes with his brothers and sister. His family of three sculptors and five artists was already famous in Canada for collaborating on the National War

◀ OPPOSITE The larger-than-life-sized statue of the Governor General who gave his name to Stanley Park looks like a miniature among these giants.

The unveiling of the Lord Stanley statue took place in May 1960, seventy-one years after the park's namesake dedicated Stanley Park.

▶ OPPOSITE The alpha tree for the Lord Stanley statue is a Douglas-fir.

Memorial of Canada, which was eventually installed in Ottawa in 1939. You can watch a short 1924 film online called *Sister and Seven Brothers Sculptors*, which shows how each family member had his or her own artistic specialty.[1]

Sydney March was eighty-four when he completed the Lord Stanley statue. I like to think he had help!

Governor General Georges Vanier, a mere seventy-two years old at the time, unveiled March's Lord Stanley statue on May 19, 1960, a rainy day.

To the use and enjoyment of people of all colours,
creeds and customs for all time.
I name thee Stanley Park.
LORD STANLEY
GOVERNOR GENERAL
OCTOBER 1889

The statue is set on a column within a grove of trees. The tallest tree, a Douglas-fir a little to the northwest of the statue, was growing when this area first became a park. It is the alpha tree for the area. It is like a local guardian, ensuring that it has Lord Stanley's back.

Yellow witch hazel flowers among evergreen azalea leaves.

Grouped beside and behind this tall Douglas-fir are several western redcedars. On one side is a large maple. A witch hazel tree brightens January days with its wispy yellow flowers. Lower to the ground, all around, are rhododendrons—some with pink flowers, some with huge glossy leaves—and an azalea. Several smaller shrubs fill in the spaces. Much of this planting was intentional.

There's an inviting bench to the southwest of Lord Stanley's outstretched arms. It is below one of the many bigleaf maples. In May, this maple is heavy with its bunches of paired seeds, its helicopters, ready to fall and give birth to more of these glorious, spreading trees with their platter-sized leaves.

Behind the statue of Lord Stanley is a playground. Between the two is a dark group of black pines (*Pinus nigra*)—one young, one middle-aged, and one fully mature and almost as tall as the Douglas-fir. Perhaps these were planted at the same time that the two rows of Austrian (or Corsican) pines were planted as a backdrop behind the Stanley Park Zoo (see chapter 16). Pine needles fall to the ground in pairs and cones lie on the grass, like woody gifts, waiting. A large-leaf linden (*Tilia platyphyllos*) hangs over the path to the west of our park's patron. More lindens grow to the east.

All the native coniferous and deciduous trees around this statue could have been here, alive and thriving, when the park was first named back in 1888. The rhododendrons have clearly been planted here, but I wonder when. Were any of these plants growing in the garden of the first park ranger, Henry Avison, and his second wife, Kate? Or were they planted here in Emily and George Eldon's garden? Or were they planted after Major Matthews came across the letter, the promise to erect a statue, and after it was decided to put the statue here and have it unveiled on May 19, 1960, by Governor General Georges Vanier, a man who hadn't even been born when the event took place?

When Lord Stanley dedicated the park, he stood on a small platform at Chaythoos (see chapter 33), clear across the park on a grassy bank near an Indigenous dwelling, above what is now the northeasterly part of the seawall. Instead, his statue is at the entrance to the park, to welcome people of all colours, creeds, and customs for all time into the majesty of this treed space.

29

The Grounds of Vancouver Park Board's Offices

The entities that are Stanley Park's trees keep busy in winter by
suspending raindrops from their branches like millions of tiny lights.

Margo Bates, event manager for Bright Nights in Stanley Park from 1997 to 2011

WHEN GEORGE ELDON was the park ranger from 1896 to 1903, he and his wife lived in the park ranger's house at the Georgia Street entrance to the park. In 1904, George became the first Park Board superintendent, and in January 1906, a new two-storey log house was built for him by the Park Board at 2099 Beach Avenue for the extravagant sum of $1,500. It had a generous yard front and back, with many young trees. I'll come back to them.

That house became home for a series of families as one superintendent retired and another took his place. A. Balmer and family lived there from 1910 to 1913 and W.S. Rawlings and family from 1913 to 1936. After a while, the house became an arts and crafts house, until November 1959, when the 53-year-old log house was demolished and the space cleared for the new Vancouver Park Board offices. Park Board staff no longer had enough space in their offices above the Stanley Park Pavilion for administering the care of more than seventy parks throughout Vancouver, a terrific undertaking. Even now, in the twenty-first century, the Vancouver Park Board is unique for its accomplishments and "the only elected body of its kind in Canada."[1]

The demolition of the old log house for the Park Board superintendent was done carefully. So carefully, in fact, that some beautiful trees—I consider them to be legacy trees—continue to surround the new low-rise Vancouver Park Board offices that were built in a West Coast "Modernist post-and-beam design idiom" in 1962.[2]

Canada's Historic Places website lists the "landscape elements":[3]

- Significant row of deciduous trees to the west,
- Espaliered Atlantic cedar at the south entry,
- Curvilinear planting beds containing both native and introduced plant material,
- Tree and shrub entryway planting, curved paths and lawn areas.

Evidently, the espaliered blue Atlas cedar (*Cedrus atlantica* 'Glauca') was planted and trained beside the building's front entrance when the Vancouver Park Board office grounds were being landscaped. When, I wonder, were some of the other legacy trees planted? Several of them have gained great height and girth, suggesting quite an age. Might these aged trees be the young ones in the image of the log house where the succession of park superintendents lived? It seems likely.

Among these very old trees are the immense European beech (*Fagus sylvatica*)

ABOVE In late fall, an espaliered blue Atlas cedar on the wall of the Vancouver Park Board offices is flanked on either side by blooming plants of *Berberis ×
hortensis*.

RIGHT A common Japanese maple grows in front of the Vancouver Park Board offices.

at the south corner of the lot, the giant sequoia (*Sequoiadendron giganteum*) along the path to the southwest, and the weeping beech (*Fagus sylvatica* 'Pendula') farther along the path.

Many of the other landscape specimens were added later. These include the English walnut (*Juglans regia*) in the east corner, the ornamental maples surrounding the entrance to parking at the back of the building (looking glorious from season to season in shades of green to every shade of red), the banana plant that benefits from the heat of the building while also getting the sunrise every morning, and the several southern magnolias (*Magnolia grandiflora*) along the northwest side of the building. Also on that northwest side are a wheel tree (*Trochodendron aralioides*), a stunning Japanese white pine (*Pinus parviflora*) heavy with cones, and an umbrella pine (*Sciadopitys verticillata*).

To the west is a group of four cut-leaf birches (*Betula pendula* 'Dalecarlica'). Planted some years after the Canadian song "Land of the Silver Birch" moved into the folk lexicon, this intimate grove whispers up its own

TOP A group of four cut-leaf birches (*Betula pendula* 'Dalecarlica') , a.k.a. Swedish birches, within the Vancouver Park Board's grounds.

BOTTOM The same group of birches within the Vancouver Park Board's grounds after a snowfall.

ABOVE Left to right, a red oak and a common Japanese maple grow on the south side of Park Lane; the Douglas-fir between the two grows on the north side.

▶ OPPOSITE The same red oak on the west corner of the Vancouver Park Board office grounds.

secrets when the wind blows in gently from English Bay.

And on the west corner of the lot is the red oak described at the end of chapter 23 (see page 165). That oak links some of the older trees with some of the newer ones.

30

Ted and Mary Greig
Rhododendron Garden

*[In 1966] the Parks Board bought the entire rhododendron collection of
the Royston Nursery, which contained some 7,000 plants and several
thousand seedlings. The Royston Nursery was owned by Ted and Mary
Greig who sold the rhododendrons to the City of Vancouver for about
one-fifth their value; in effect, the plants were a gift.*

"The Trees and Shrubs of Stanley Park: English Bay to Lost Lagoon," Don Benson and
Alleyne Cook, in *The Natural History of Stanley Park*, Vancouver Natural History Society

THE PUTTING GREEN (see chapter 23), with its native and exotic trees,
attracted putters from 1920 onwards. Another twelve years passed
before a par-three golf course—the Stanley Park Pitch & Putt—was
completed in 1932 to the northeast of the putting green. The course's
eighteen holes are built carefully around some mature trees that were
already growing in the region.

In the evenings, the place was quiet. Hoping to make the path
around the Pitch & Putt a safe place for people to stroll by day and at
dusk, the Park Board decided to make the area a showpiece of ornamental shrubs and trees. Park Board commissioners voted to buy Ted
and Mary Greig's collection of hybridized rhododendrons and azaleas
in 1966, and hired Alleyne Cook, a rhododendron expert, to arrange
for the transportation of the Greigs' life's work from the east coast of
Vancouver Island to the mainland. A master gardener, Cook then created the landscape design for these beauties.

◄ OPPOSITE
A cotoneaster's bright
red pomes brighten up
approaching winter on
the Pitch & Putt.

The Pitch & Putt is colourful in the fall.

Several signs in the southwest corner of Stanley Park announce that you have arrived at the Ted and Mary Greig Rhododendron Garden. It mostly surrounds the Pitch & Putt course. Nowadays, the area is hugely popular.

Of the seven thousand plants the Park Board bought from the Greigs at their retirement, four and a half thousand are now growing well in Stanley Park; the rest are flourishing in Queen Elizabeth Park and VanDusen Garden, two other Vancouver city parks.

I don't know much about the genus of *Rhododendron* and its 1,024 species of plants in the heath family, Ericaceae.[1] I do know that rhododendrons attract specialists within the world of botany, and that among these botanical specialists, the Greigs rank very high. A plaque along the main path of the rhododendron walk honours them.

Dedicated to Ted and Mary Greig, pioneers in Rhododendron culture in British Columbia. They were awarded a gold medal by the American Rhododendron Society in 1965. The Greigs established a nursery at Royston on Vancouver Island in 1935. Their Rhododendron collection was acquired by the Vancouver Park Board in 1966. Some of the Greig hybrids in this garden are unique in that they combine fragrance with mid-summer bloom, both rare qualities in Rhododendrons.

THIS PLAQUE DEDICATED JUNE, 1989.

VANCOUVER RHODODENDRON SOCIETY

Stanley Park is indebted to Ted and Mary Greig and their generosity.

The decadent trusses of light orange or mauve or freckled pale pink or ruby-red rhododendron flowers make the Ted and Mary Greig Rhododendron Garden one of the most popular areas of Stanley Park from March to September.

Azaleas comprise two subgenera (*Pentanthera* and *Tsutsusi*) of flowering shrubs in the *Rhododendron* genus; they are rhododendrons, but they differ from "true" rhododendrons by having five or six stamens per flower rather than ten or more, as rhododendrons have. They also grow flowers singly or in groups of up to three together at the end of a stem. Some azaleas are deciduous and some are evergreen.

Rhododendrons, on the other hand, are mostly evergreen. They range between being shrubs and trees, each flower has ten or more stamens, and their flowers grow together in large clusters that resemble bouquets and are called trusses.

Cook planted rhodos and some three hundred and fifty azaleas around the entire circumference of the Pitch & Putt, making the border of the golf course one of the most cultivated areas of Stanley Park, indeed "one of Vancouver's finest collection of trees, shrubs, and garden flowers."[2] In 1979, as part of his final landscaping, Cook planted seven rhododendron beds as the medians between the fairways inside the course itself.

Map and Walking Order of Azaleas and Rhododendrons

If you would like to identify the rhododendron and azalea cultivars in this part of Stanley Park, download the Park Board's three PDFs about this area.[3] The documents are organized to show the main walks (Magnolia, Azalea, and Camellia), and the plants are listed alphabetically by species. To make it easier for non-botanists, I have redone the two maps and the plants by genus or species, cultivar, and walking order, going counter-clockwise around the Pitch & Putt.

Trees Other Than Rhododendrons in the Rhododendron Garden

Many trees other than rhododendrons were planted in the Ted and Mary Greig Rhododendron Garden.

WEST END BORDER The first area where Cook began planting in 1966 was a slim piece of the park that runs between Beach Avenue and Nelson Street: the West End Border (trees 1 to 13 in the map on page 226). It is sandwiched between Park Lane and the West End and spills over toward the Pitch & Putt. There is an inviting path connecting Comox Street with Park Lane that is a frequent route for West Enders who are walking through this area to the horse chestnut triangle or the bowling greens or the tennis courts or the Pitch & Putt. From early spring until late fall, some-

Walking Order of Azaleas and Rhododendrons

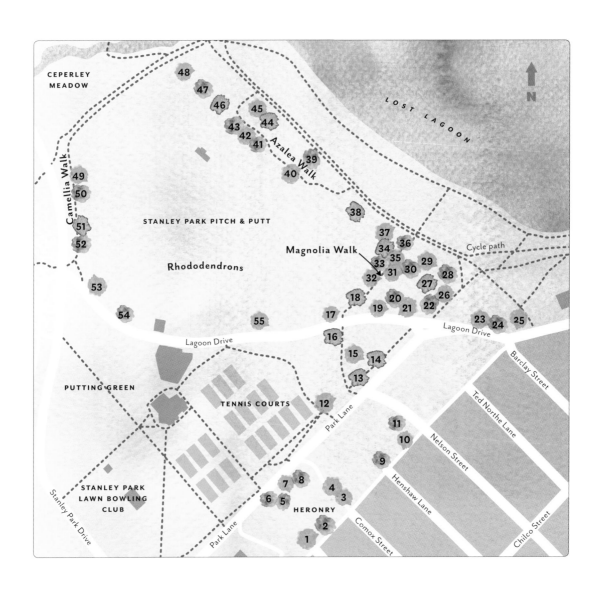

1. *Rhododendron* 'Chionoides'
2. *Rhododendron* 'Mrs. A.T. de la Mare'
3. *Rhododendron smirnowii*
4. *Rhododendron* 'Fastuosum Flore Pleno'
5. *Rhododendron* 'Fabia'
6. *Rhododendron* 'Susan'
7. *Rhododendron* 'Beethoven'
8. *Rhododendron* 'Naomi Hope'
9. *Rhododendron* 'Impi'
10. *Rhododendron augustinii*
11. *Rhododendron* 'Anna Rose Whitney'
12. *Rhododendron* 'The Honourable Jean Marie de Montague'
13. *Rhododendron* 'Anna Rose Whitney'
14. *Rhododendron* 'Sappho'
15. *Rhododendron* 'Beauty of Littleworth'
16. *Rhododendron* 'Fabia'
17. *Rhododendron* 'Purple Splendor'
18. *Rhododendron* 'Fabia'
19. *Rhododendron* 'Yellow Hammer'
20. *Rhododendron* 'Point Defiance'
21. *Rhododendron ambiguum*
22. *Rhododendron* 'Electra'
23. *Rhododendron* 'Cunningham's White'
24. *Rhododendron decorum*
25. *Rhododendron auriculatum*
26. *Rhododendron* 'May Day'
27. *Rhododendron cinnabarinum*
28. *Rhododendron* 'Cilpinense'
29. *Rhododendron* 'Elizabeth'
30. *Rhododendron occidentale*
31. *Rhododendron* 'Haydn'
32. *Rhododendron* 'Aladdin'
33. *Rhododendron* 'Azor'
34. *Rhododendron augustinii*
35. *Rhododendron* 'George Watling'
36. *Rhododendron* 'Palestrina'
37. *Rhododendron* 'Wedding Present'
38. *Rhododendron* 'Whitney's Orange'
39. *Rhododendron* 'Unique'
40. *Rhododendron* 'Royston Red'
41. *Rhododendron auriculatum*
42. *Rhododendron atlanticum*
43. *Rhododendron arboreum*
44. *Rhododendron* 'President Roosevelt'
45. *Rhododendron* 'Naomi Nautilus'
46. *Rhododendron* 'Crest'
47. *Rhododendron* 'Beauty of Littleworth'
48. *Rhododendron* 'Lady Clementine Mitford'
49. *Rhododendron* 'Moonstone'
50. *Rhododendron* 'Scintillation'
51. *Rhododendron* 'Bonfire'
52. *Rhododendron schlippenbachii*
53. *Rhododendron* 'Mrs. Furnival'
54. *Rhododendron* 'Baden Baden'
55. *Rhododendron fortunei*

Common Japanese maple (*Acer palmatum*) and beautyberry (*Callicarpa bodinieri giraldii*) add colour to the path.

Peeling bark of paperbark maple (*Acer griseum*).

A China fir (*Cunninghamia lanceolata*) shows fresh, light green growth.

thing is flowering within this border of the park, either the beautyberry (*Callicarpa bodinieri giraldii*) or one of the ornamental cherry trees. Also of interest are the paperbark maples (*Acer griseum*) and a China fir (*Cunninghamia lanceolata*).

Having spent the entire year's plant budget on rhododendrons in 1966, Park Board gardeners had to display some ingenuity in securing trees for this area. One year, Alleyne Cook consulted with English ornithologist, plant collector, and gardener Collingwood "Cherry" Ingram. Cherry had gained a reputation as the world's authority on flowering cherries. Acting on Cherry's advice, Alleyne sent to the Hillier Garden Centre in Winchester, England, for six particular ornamental cherry trees, which he then used as the basis for propagating more

ornamental cherries at a tree nursery in Chilliwack, in the Fraser Valley. In groups of five, these trees were planted where needed.

Another year, working with Art Fulawka, who was in charge of Vancouver Park Board's forestry crew, Alleyne purchased the only one of ten giant dogwoods (*Cornus controversa*) to survive a particularly cold winter. It has the specific name of *controversa* because of its controversial nature of having alternately arranged leaves, unlike most members of the *Cornus* genus, which has oppositely arranged leaves.

A *Cornus kousa*, a dogwood that blooms in late July and into August, thereby extending the dogwood flowering season through the summer, flourishes, grows tall, and spreads wide near Pooh Corner Day Care. The kousa dogwood is easy to recognize by

ABOVE From its emergence each spring, the Brazilian giant-rhubarb (*Gunnera manicata*) plant reaches its full height in September; there are several such plants in different locations within the Greig Rhododendron Garden.

RIGHT Deciduous fronds of baldcypress (*Taxodium distichum*) are preparing to fall as the days get cooler.

Walking Order of Trees in Ted and Mary Greig Rhododendron Garden

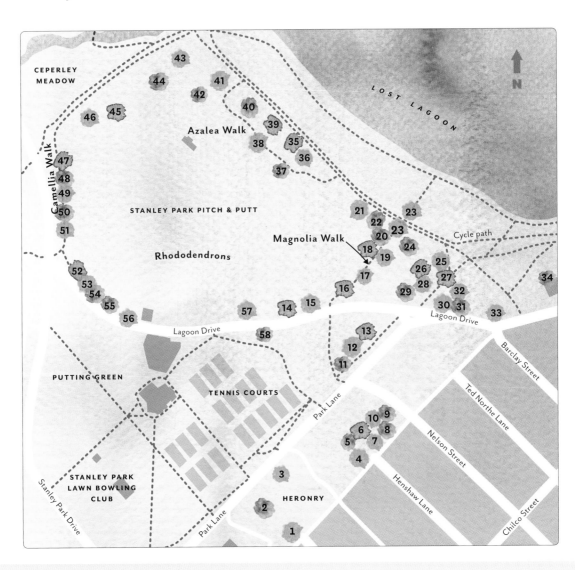

A Lanarth viburnum

West End Border

1. Silk tassel bush (*Garrya elliptica*)

2. China fir (*Cunninghamia lanceolata*)

3. Beautyberry (*Callicarpa bodinieri giraldii*)

4. Paperbark maple (*Acer griseum*)

5. Hungarian oak (*Quercus frainetto* 'Forest Green')

6. Jeffrey pine (*Pinus jeffreyi*), a.k.a. yellow pine

7. Antarctic beech (*Nothofagus antarctica*)

8. Vilmorin's rowan (*Sorbus vilmorinii*)

9. Mountain laurel (*Kalmia latifolia*), a.k.a. calico-bush and spoonwood, more of a shrub

10. Delavay tea olive (*Osmanthus delavayi*)

11. Persian silk tree (*Albizia julibrissin*), a.k.a. pink silk tree and mimosa

12. Variegated pagoda dogwood (*Cornus alternifolia* 'Argentea')

13. Ponderosa pine (*Pinus ponderosa*), a.k.a. bull pine, blackjack pine, and western yellow-pine

Magnolia Walk

14. Pink-flowering dogwood (*Cornus florida* 'Rubra')

15. Siebold's magnolia (*Magnolia sieboldii*), a.k.a. Korean mountain magnolia and Oyama magnolia

16. Japanese cucumber tree (*Magnolia hypoleuca*)

17. Wilson's magnolia (*Magnolia wilsonii*)

18. Umbrella tree (*Magnolia tripetala*)

19. Yellow lantern magnolia (*Magnolia* 'Yellow Lantern,' a.k.a. *M. acuminata* var. subcordata × *M. × soulangeana* 'Alexandrina')

20. Giant dogwood (*Cornus controversa*)

21. Tulip tree (*Liriodendron tulipifera*), a.k.a. yellow poplar

22. Dove tree (*Davidia involucrata*), a.k.a. handkerchief tree, pocket handkerchief tree, and ghost tree

23. Dawn redwood (*Metasequoia glyptostroboides*); there are two of these, one on each side of the path, like sentinels with straight trunks unlike the braided trunks of the dawn redwoods described on page 178

24. Barbara Cook magnolia (*Magnolia dawsoniana* 'Barbara Cook')

25. Dawson's magnolia (*Magnolia dawsoniana*)

26. Orange ball buddleia (*Buddleja globosa*), a.k.a. orange-ball-tree

27. Elderberry (*Sambucus racemosa*)

28. Princess tree (*Paulownia tomentosa*), a.k.a. foxglove tree

29. Japanese stuartia (*Stewartia pseudocamellia*)

30. Common laburnum (*Laburnum anagyroides*), a.k.a. golden chain tree and golden rain

31. Dead man's fingers (*Decaisnea fargesii*), a.k.a. blue bean plant and blue sausage fruit

32. Wheel tree (*Trochodendron aralioides*)

33. Amur cork tree (*Phellodendron amurense*)

34. Kousa dogwood (*Cornus kousa*)

Azalea Walk

35. Brazilian giant-rhubarb (*Gunnera manicata*), a.k.a. dinosaur food

36. California laurel (*Umbellularia californica*)

37. Golden raintree (*Koelreuteria paniculata*)

38. February daphne (*Daphne mezereum*)

39. Redvein enkianthus (*Enkianthus campanulatus*)

40. Princess tree (*Paulownia tomentosa*), a.k.a. foxglove tree

41. Lanarth viburnum (*Viburnum plicatum* 'Lanarth'), a.k.a. Japanese snowball

42. Ukon flowering cherry (*Prunus serrulata* 'Ukon')

43. Baldcypress (*Taxodium distichum*)

44. Wheel tree (*Trochodendron aralioides*)

45. Katsura (*Cercidiphyllum japonicum*)

46. Donation camellia (*Camellia × williamsii* 'Donation')

Camellia Walk

47. Sweetbay magnolia (*Magnolia virginiana*)

48. Tea plant (*Camellia sinensis*)

49. Alternate-leaved butterfly bush (*Buddleja alternifolia*), a.k.a. buddleia

50. Saucer magnolia (*Magnolia × soulangeana*)

51. Harlequin glorybower (*Clerodendrum trichotomum*)

Pitch & Putt Southern Boundary

52. Maidenhair tree (*Ginkgo biloba*)

53. Fragrant snowbell (*Styrax obassia*)

54. Chinese winter hazel (*Corylopsis sinensis*)

55. Korean-spice viburnum (*Viburnum carlesii*)

56. Princess tree (*Paulownia tomentosa*), a.k.a. foxglove tree

57. Tanoak (*Notholithocarpus densiflorus*), a.k.a. tanbark oak

58. Kobus magnolia (*Magnolia kobus*)

Edible fruit of kousa dogwood

its large, red, edible berries that resemble strawberries. Tasting rather like a soft pear, the fruit pulp is very soft and filled with seeds that can break a tooth. Be careful!

When I took the Lagoon Drive sidewalk beside the Pitch & Putt in early April 2018, I was astounded by the abundance of immensely tall kobus magnolias. Their flowers are almost identical to those of a star magnolia, but kobus magnolias are tall and showy, whereas a star magnolia is usually a shrub or a small tree. Planted strategically throughout the gardens as an intentional link, they clearly love the temperature and soil conditions here in Stanley Park.

Like many of the park's unsung heroes, Alleyne Cook is to be thanked for the twenty-two years he dedicated to this area of Stanley Park. He hybridized some magnolias during this time, one being the 'Barbara Cook' magnolia (*Magnolia dawsoniana* 'Barbara Cook'). Planted near a Dawson's magnolia that has a spread of some one hundred feet, the 'Barbara Cook' blossoms a vibrant pink in early spring. Asked why he named the hybrid for his wife, Barbara, Alleyne said it was because the magnolia, like his wife, is the first in its class.[4]

31

Second Beach and Ceperley Field and Meadow

Trees embody and are embodied in their native ecologies.
They tell us much about those ecologies and the world.
If we listen.

M. Ross Waddell, a founder of the Native Plant Society of British Columbia

ONE OF THE most popular areas in Stanley Park these days is at Second Beach, with its swimming pool, its two playgrounds, and the level green of Ceperley Field, which runs the length of the beach. Farther to the east is a wilder area known as Ceperley Meadow. The area's native ecology has changed considerably.

Untouched to the north of the natural beach, though, is a native stand of western redcedars, their scent intoxicating.

At one time, there was a bathhouse and a pier at Second Beach. It was a great place to go for a ride in the buggy, to meet for a picnic, to climb over foreshore rocks and sand lenses, and to have a swim.

In 1907, the Park Board installed six swings at Second Beach.[1] This was the first children's playground anywhere in Stanley Park.

But for the generosity of early park commissioners, the work of managing Stanley Park might have gone unpaid more often. Park commissioner Alfred Graham Ferguson[2]—the A.G. Ferguson for whom Ferguson Point is named—reimbursed suppliers on a number of occasions.

◄ OPPOSITE Path down to Second Beach.

The forest in the 1910s at Second Beach.

Mr. Ferguson . . . took such an interest in Stanley Park that, when the annual sum appropriated by the Council for its upkeep and development was exhausted, he himself invariably paid the bills to the end of the year. Being a civil engineer, he gave the grades for grading the roads in the park, acted as park foreman, and practically gave all his spare time to it, the other commissioners being agreeable to leaving it to him . . .

Mr. Ferguson left a portion of his estate to his [sister] Mrs. Ceperley, with the suggestion that, when she had no further use for it, it should be left to the city of Vancouver, and this gave us, ultimately, the Ceperley Children's Playground at Second Beach. I believe Mr. Ferguson stipulated in his bequest that the money should be used for a park for children."[3]

The dedication plaque at Ceperley Playground, 180 metres southeast of the

original six-swings playground, reads as follows:

This playground was equipped by the late Mrs. Grace E. Ceperley and dedicated to the Board of Park Commissioners for the use and benefit of the children of the City of Vancouver

JUNE 14, 1924

A few of the trees bounding the area around the dedicated playground were probably planted at the time the playground equipment was first installed. One is an extremely tall, widely spreading pin oak (*Quercus palustris*). Others are a London plane tree, a horse chestnut, and a member

of the walnut family, perhaps a black walnut (*Juglans nigra*). What a perfect place to plant a bank of trees to shade children and parents alike.

I am grateful to Alfred Ferguson and his sister Grace Ceperley for bequeathing the initial playground equipment, though the playground has changed over the years. A retired red fire engine was installed in 1967, which all my grandchildren have "driven."[4] No matter the day, small people and their parents are always on the move here.

In the 1930s and '40s, the Park Board opened a saltwater swimming pool and a paddling pool at Second Beach, but saltwater corrodes pipes and neither pool lasted

The Boy Scouts and Cubs Rally gathers on Ceperley Field for the visit of Governor General Lord Bessborough on September 7, 1932.

Boys are mastering the three-finger salute used by scout and guide organizations the world over to honour the presence of Governor General Lord Tweedsmuir in 1936, the year he also opened the Shakespeare Garden in Stanley Park.

A European ash (*Fraxinus excelsior*) near the road and bike path between Ceperley Field and Ceperley Meadows.

Cyclists take the path through Ceperley Field.

TOP A linden tree (*Tilia platyphyllos*) in bloom.

BOTTOM Red sunset backlights willows and a deodar cedar.

long. These days, there is a freshwater swimming pool, a concession stand, and no pier—change aplenty.

The forest itself in the region of Second Beach has changed completely. The original native maples, western redcedars, Douglas-firs, and red alders have been cleared so that ceremonies, sports, and parades could be held on this flat ground.

Where once there was forest, rows of planted trees now surround the cleared space that is Ceperley Field. In the east and the northeast corner are European ash (*Fraxinus excelsior*), which turn a striking yellow in fall. Weeping willows (*Salix* 'Chrysocoma') are in the northwest corner near the swimming pool,

The skeleton of a tree that crows loved to frequent is no longer in the grounds of the swimming pool at Second Beach.

and two rows of linden trees (*Tilia platyphyllos*) and maples are on the west side. Inside the swimming pool fence, alongside a couple of arbutus trees, there used to be a skeleton of a tree that crows loved to frequent. It's now gone.

In the southwest corner, overlooking the southerly playground, is a memorial to those who died in the bombing of Air India Flight 182 on June 23, 1985, an act of terrorism that killed 331 people.

This memorial honours the 329 passengers and crew who perished in the bombing of Air India Flight 182 on June 23rd, 1985, at 0713 G.M.T.

off the coast of Ireland, and the two baggage
handlers killed in the associated bombing at
Narita Airport in Japan on that day.

This act of terrorism is a Canadian tragedy,
planned and executed on Canadian soil.
The Government of Canada has declared
June 23rd to be a national day of remembrance
for victims of terrorism.

This wall, symbolic of the flight path, terminates
with a stone from Ahakista, Ireland.

The stones below are from all of the places
directly affected by this tragedy.

The curved wall and the leaning monument holding the memorial plaques are positioned around a handsome London plane tree. Behind the wall are three healthy young dove trees (*Davidia involucrata*), planted in July 2007 to add shade and solemnity to the memorial. This tree species owes its reputation as a beauty to its pairs of gently hanging white bracts that surround each spring flower. It is also known as a handkerchief tree or a ghost tree.

Returning northwest to the original playground area, we pass a mugo pine (*Pinus mugo*), a deodar cedar, and a row of weeping willows.

If you leave Ceperley Field and head east, you reach Ceperley Meadow—a wilder place where ducks dive when temporary pools appear, herons wait for lunch, and beaver can sometimes be seen searching for suitable fodder trees. Ceperley Meadow links Ceperley Field with the path around Lost Lagoon and the Ted and Mary Greig Rhododendron Garden.

On the north side of the Ceperley Meadow path, opposite a small wooden bridge over Ceperley Stream, you will find the Peace Train Tree (latitude 49.2958 N | longitude 123.1472 W). North Lagoon Drive is to the north.

The Peace Train Tree plaque reads,

On this day, the 7th of July, 1988, Soviet and
Canadian children from the Peace Train,

The memorial to the bombing of Air India Flight 182 in 1985 is at the south corner of Ceperley Field. It is surrounded by trees.

in cooperation with the Vancouver Board of Parks and Recreation, planted this 12' silver birch to unite our two countries in peace and friendship, and to recall for future generations that peace, like trees, needs time and care to grow.

When I visited the Peace Train birch last, I pulled an invasive Himalayan blackberry off its lowest branch. I also noticed that sapsuckers—a North American woodpecker genus—had pecked several rows of holes into the trunks. The holes made by sapsuckers cause sap to run, inviting small bugs into the mix, making for a delicious meal for a woodpecker. Otherwise, the birch looked healthy and was protected with wire netting from the beavers that are active around Lost Lagoon.

Birch trees grow prolifically in both Canada (just think of the folk song "Land of the Silver Birch") and Russia (the folk song "Beriozka" is often translated as "There Was a Birch Tree in the Field").

This birch, with its white bark cracked into black patches in places, is a double-trunked specimen. It's a silver birch (*Betula pendula*). I wondered at first whether the trunk had split after the tree had been planted. According to *The Hidden Life of Trees* by Peter Wohlleben, trees with a split at ground level have an extra challenge in surviving to maturity. But later, I heard from a

◀ OPPOSITE
Ceperley Meadow
early one morning.

LEFT A glimpse
of Ceperley Meadow
from Stanley Park Drive.

RIGHT Ceperley Meadow.

A heron waits patiently in Ceperley Meadow.

Both trunks of the Peace Train Tree show sapsucker damage.

Ceperley Stream sometimes ices over in winter.

park planner that landscape architects like to plant double-trunked birches because they see twice as much peeling bark for the price of one tree.

Though not every birch tree has peeling bark, every birch does have doubly serrate-toothed, alternately arranged leaves—a good method for genus identification.

32

The Holly and the Ivy
and the Monkey Puzzle Trees

The holly and the ivy,
When they are both full grown
Of all the trees that are in the wood
The holly bears the crown

Traditional British folk song

DO YOU REMEMBER the early photograph of the Oppenheimer bust (see page 100), with a monkey puzzle tree (*Araucaria araucana*) growing behind it?

Well, the picture overleaf is of the Stanley Park statue commemorating the Scottish "Bard of Ayrshire" Robert Burns and his poetry. This Jack Lindsay photograph taken between 1940 and 1948 captures both the full-grown monkey puzzle tree and the Robbie Burns statue.

The 2.8-metre bronze figure standing atop a granite pedestal (at latitude 49.2972 | longitude 123.1347 W) is a replica of a statue designed by George Lawson in Ayr, County Ayrshire, Scotland. (Burns himself was born 3 kilometres south of Ayr, to a tenant-farming family.) The replica, which cost $5,000 in the late 1920s, was shipped to Vancouver via the Panama Canal.[1] The unveiling of this statue gathered large crowds in 1928.

The Seaforth Highlanders of Canada, Vancouver's Reserve Infantry regiment, grouped in front of this statue in 1929 to have their picture taken, showing how the Scottish diaspora loved their bard.

TOP Notice the monkey puzzle tree behind the commemorative statue of Robert Burns.

BOTTOM The unveiling of the statue of Robert Burns gathered big crowds in 1928.

Like the monkey puzzle tree behind the Oppenheimer bust, the Robert Burns monkey puzzle tree has gone. Instead, the closest tree to that statue is a giant sequoia (*Sequoiadendron giganteum*), an evergreen with small overlapping scales. I don't know enough to guess its age.

Did the monkey puzzle tree die of some disease that's unknown in its native Chile and Argentina? Did it succumb to all our rain? Or—and I think this is the most likely reason—did it go out of vogue?

If you walk along the shoulder of land northeast of the statue, you will see several stumps of trees cut very low to the ground. These stumps are sprouting new growth, energetically, in the way this species does: it's English holly, much revered in the Christmas carol that opens this chapter. Clearly, these English holly trees were planted to commemorate Robert Burns's British origin. Why were they cut down? I'll hazard a guess shortly.

When the early park rangers began caretaking these thousand acres of forested

A giant sequoia (with a lean from the parallax effect of the camera) and some linden trees grow around the Robert Burns statue now, in place of the monkey puzzle tree and holly trees that were planted around it originally.

parkland, they brought with them their British and European values. They planted English holly and English ivy. Somehow, seeds of the Himalayan blackberry piggybacked in with the soil around transported plants. The first park ranger caught and tethered brown bears. Park caretakers fenced off small paddocks for bison, emu, and elk. They displayed penguins, monkeys, and polar bears for the entertainment of the public.

I was one such voyeur. On my first visit from Cardiff to Vancouver in 1961, I was fascinated by the monkeys who could swing by their tails from one high railing to another. I naively didn't care that monkeys weren't native to Canada.

The Park Board even purchased enough pairs of eastern grey squirrels (*Sciurus carolinensis*) for the introduced species to populate the park and make the new European residents of Vancouver feel at home. That was in 1914, over a hundred years ago. Non-native bullfrogs, green frogs, and red-eared slider turtles have also found their way into the park.

Mute swans, natives of Eurasia, were introduced to the park and frequently fed

by visitors to Lost Lagoon. In the 1970s, they numbered more than eighty. They would chase away the native trumpeter swans that stopped over on their journey south in the winter or north in the summer.

In 1988, as part of Stanley Park's centennial celebrations, the Stanley Park Ecology Society (SPES) was formed. Actually, its original name was the Stanley Park Zoological Society (SPZS), but following the yes-let's-close-the-Stanley-Park-Zoo referendum vote in 1994, SPZS changed its name. SPES's mission is to promote "awareness of and respect for the natural world and [play] a leadership role in the stewardship of Stanley Park through collaborative initiatives in education, research and conservation."[2]

The park had gained a conscience. And a yardstick by which to choose its activities, the ones that would "maintain and restore Stanley Park's ecosystems."

This is how English holly trees fell out of favour. It's easy to see why. They don't belong in Stanley Park. Cultivated holly trees can grow into luxurious, deep green specimens of prickly leaves, impervious to wind and weather. "The holly bears the crown." The song is referring to the crown of thorns that was placed on Jesus's head at his crucifixion.

Female holly trees (only one in ten is female) bear a small, bright red fruit. Brits love to bring a small sprig of holly into their home at Christmastime to celebrate the season. Birds love this bright red fruit, too. The problem is that birds fly away with the berry's hard seed in their gizzard. When the bird poops in the forest, the undigested fertilized seed lands on the ground in a small package of nourishment that helps it get established. Wild, escaped holly is now sprouting up all over the park in unwanted places. And so, the female holly trees had to go, though there are still some growing untouched.

I suspect that monkey puzzle trees also fell victim to such a healthy conscience in an earlier time, though there is one lone survivor standing quite tall beside the east lane of traffic at the park entrance to the Lions Gate Bridge. Perhaps it was planted at the time of the opening of the bridge in 1938; it *is* quite tall.

Another role involving SPES is the shrinking of Beaver Lake, one of Vancouver's "last remaining wetlands."[3] Together with the Park Board, SPES developed habitat restoration plans to ensure the lake does not continue to infill, which is due in part to the proliferation of invasive water lilies, planted for a visit from a member of the British royal family that never materialized.

The Invasive Species Council of BC coordinated an Invasive Species Strategy for the province with input from more than a hundred agencies, organizations, businesses, and residents.[4] The list of invasives includes the eastern grey squirrel, American bullfrog, English holly, English ivy (*Hedera helix*), and Himalayan blackberry.

◄ OPPOSITE Beaver Lake is situated at latitude 49.304 N | longitude 123.14 W, and can be accessed from the north, south, and east. A walking path surrounds the lake.

Vancouver Park Board employees have their work cut out, which is why they have teamed up with SPES to restore Stanley Park's ecosystems. One of SPES's most hands-on laborious activities is the removal of ivy and Himalayan blackberry from the park. SPES welcomes volunteers of all ages and abilities.[5] Atlantic ivy (*Hedera hibernica*), sometimes known as Irish ivy and erroneously as English ivy, is an invasive plant that has taken over in parts of the park; like English ivy, it uses its aerial roots to climb up and eventually smother its host trees, stopping them from capturing sufficient sunlight to convert into essential, energizing chlorophyll.

Fashions fluctuate, our climate is changing, and our ideas of what does and doesn't belong in Stanley Park evolve. While there may seem to be a constant backdrop of trees, bushes, and groundcover as we walk through the park, once we become more aware, we may see the subtle changes.

33

Two Trees at Chaythoos

Each tree in the forest is a treasure
This Western redcedar was planted as a gift to the future on Stanley
Park's 125th Anniversary September 27, 2013
City of Vancouver / Vancouver Board of Parks and Recreation /
Stanley Park

Engraved below a western redcedar at Chaythoos

THERE ARE TWO young trees at Chaythoos, the Squamish name for the area where Mayor David Oppenheimer opened Stanley Park and Lord Stanley dedicated it. Each of these trees has a story.

City archivist Major Matthews and his wife and their friends, teacher Kenneth J. Waites and his wife, took a Sunday evening drive through Stanley Park four days after the coronation on Wednesday, May 12, 1937, of King George VI and Queen Elizabeth.

At the Major's suggestion, the party stopped at the Water Works Cottage at the end of Pipeline Road (3571 Stanley Park Drive) to meet its occupant, Frank Harris. Matthews had served at the Battle of Ypres alongside Harris's son Sid, a private in the 102nd Canadian Infantry Battalion, and one of the many thousands of Canadian casualties at that First World War battle.

Matthews recalled what a fine young man Frank Harris's son Sid had been. "If he had not been killed in action Sid would have risen. He might have come back from the war with almost any rank at all."[1]

The Matthewses and the Waiteses settled in for one of Major Matthews's interviews. Major Matthews, feeling he was always on duty, brought up the naming of Stanley Park by Mayor David Oppenheimer and the dedication of Stanley Park by Lord Stanley, events that had taken place a year apart, a stone's throw away from Frank Harris's cottage.

By May 1937, Frank Harris had been living in Stanley Park in the Water Works Cottage for almost fifty years, having been caretaker of the water works' interests on the Stanley Park shore since 1888. His cottage was a few steps north of an old settlement belonging to Squamish Chief Khahtsahlano—whose name was also spelled Haatsa-lah-nogh (by non-Indigenous people) and for whom Kitsilano is named. Chief Khahtsahlano went to and fro between his home in Squamish and his home in what became Stanley Park until his death in the early 1880s.

Hay-tulk, the chief's son, who was known to westerners as Supplejack, and his wife, Sally (known to many as Aunt Sally), moved from Squamish at the north end of Howe Sound to the house owned by his father. Supplejack and Sally lived there with their three children, Louisa, Cecile, and Willie Jack. Supplejack worked at Hastings Mill and died the day his youngest son, August Jack, was born, in October 1877. Supplejack's widow remarried.

This happened more than a decade before the surveyors came to lay out the road around the future park. Supplejack's burial chamber—Squamish people at that time buried their dead in a canoe surrounded by glass and covered by red blankets—was in the path of the park road. It was moved out of the way. The surveyors nicked off a corner of the house too. Later, in 1900, the Park Board bought Aunt Sally's house for the paltry sum of $25 and burned it to the ground.[2]

Let us return to Frank Harris's sitting room, where he and his wife are entertaining Major Matthews and party. Harris is speaking.

> On Wednesday . . . we planted two oaks just outside there. Jonathan Rogers [of Rogers Building, park commissioner for twenty years] planted one to mark the spot where Lord Stanley opened the park, and Mrs. Alice Townley, former park commissioner, planted the one to commemorate the coronation of King George and Queen Elizabeth. They are about ten feet high.[3]

By the time I read this statement in *Early Vancouver*, I had already come across the English oak that Alice Townley planted in the putting green (chapter 23). My next step was to find the English oak planted by Alderman Jonathan Rogers for King George VI's Coronation Day to commemorate Lord Stanley's dedication of Stanley Park. I took a good look at the map of Chaythoos that August Jack and Major Matthews compiled (I cannot link to it here because it is under copyright). I also looked online to see where the oak might be. I then started searching, looking for a tall oak the same age as the tree in the putting green. I didn't find one; granted, it was winter, so the leaves of every deciduous tree in the area had long since fallen to the ground.

What I did find was a western redcedar planted for the 125th anniversary of Stanley Park. The words on the plaque introduce this chapter.

I returned to Chaythoos in spring and walked throughout the area again, systematically. I recognized that a tree labelled on one particular website as being the "King George VI Windsor Oak Tree" is in fact a bigleaf maple—a simple matter of expectation and misidentification.

I talked to a park gardener, who suggested that the tree planted in 1937 might have been struck by lightning or become diseased. Perhaps it fell in the 2006 windstorm.

I went back to Major Matthews's *Early Vancouver* publications and found an entry of a 1941 conversation Matthews had with Frank Harris, in which Harris said, "I met an old gentleman in Stanley Park the other day . . ."

> He told me that each year for the last three years, he has planted ten pounds of acorns all about Stanley Park. A few which he must have planted earlier, he told me, are now about two-feet-high trees, oak trees. He has no permission; I don't think the park people know he is doing it, and he plants

A very young English oak tree has been planted at Chaythoos where once an English oak from Windsor Great Park was planted in memory of the naming of Stanley Park on the Coronation Day of King George VI and Queen Elizabeth.

them anywhere and everywhere. He told me that, in three years, he has set out thirty pounds of acorns, ten pounds each year, in the earth; just pushed them in anywhere.[4]

I still hoped to find the commemorative tree, so I returned yet again to Chaythoos. This time, in a slightly different location than I expected such a tree to be, I found a very young English oak tree, no more than a sapling (latitude 49.310 N | longitude 123.138 W). It's barely 2 metres tall.

I believe this young oak was planted to replace the Windsor oak planted on King George VI's Coronation Day in 1937 to commemorate Lord Stanley's dedication of Stanley Park. To remind us all that this park is for the use and enjoyment of people of all colours, creeds, and customs for all time.

I believe I have found a replacement tree for the King George VI Windsor Oak Tree. I would love to hear the story of how and why it found its way to Chaythoos. How fitting that a young tree should continue the heritage, quietly, subtly, and perseveringly honouring Stanley Park's legacy of trees.

Epilogue

The Roots of the Matter

A Rugged, Ragged, and Craggy History

THE PARK'S HISTORY is at times rugged, ragged, and craggy, tricky to tease apart, despite the dates of this and that. The park is not pristine, perfect, or always pretty. It has its dark moments of shame, immorality, and ignorance. But in the end, Stanley Park is what it is—a shared public resource, judged Best Park in the World by TripAdvisor in 2014, frequented by the world, loved by millions, and cared for by some.

I turn to Suzanne Simard, a western Canadian forester and ecologist, for encouragement. After thirty years of research, Simard has four simple solutions to the question that inspires most of her work:

How can we reinforce our forests and help them deal with climate change?…

First, we all need to get out in the forest. We need to reestablish local involvement in our own forests. You see, most of our forests now are managed using a one-size-fits-all approach, but good forest stewardship requires knowledge of local conditions.

Second, we need to save our old-growth forests. These are the repositories of genes and mother trees and mycorrhizal networks. So this means less cutting. I don't mean no cutting, but less cutting.

And third, when we do cut, we need to save the legacies, the mother trees and networks, and the wood, the genes, so they can pass their wisdom onto the next generation of trees so they can withstand the future stresses coming down the road. We need to be conservationists.

And ... fourthly and finally, we need to regenerate our forests with a diversity of species and genotypes and structures by planting and allowing natural regeneration. We have to give Mother Nature the tools she needs to use her intelligence to self-heal. And we need to remember that forests aren't just a bunch of trees competing with each other, they're supercooperators.[1]

It may seem strange to discuss cutting down trees in a public park, but even nowadays, such cutting happens for reasons of safety and disease. Stanley Park is partly an old-growth forest; it is also a playground and a place for recreation. The park is to be protected and so are the people who visit it. My hope for the future of this park is that it continues to be loved, well cared for during the upcoming changes provided by climate change, and respected for what it is: a piece of nature that humanity tries to improve upon and never can.

My Research Journey

Bit by bit, year by year, trees have been planted in Stanley Park, turning what was a selectively logged coastal forest into an urban park. There are no official city records to identify all the ornamental trees that have been planted. However, lists have been compiled, and I have been lucky enough to track down many of them. This book is an attempt to bring all these lists and records into one place.

In the early 1970s, John Yak, MD, approached the Vancouver Park Board public relations manager of the time, Terri Clark, with an invaluable list of the ornamental trees he had identified.

> A wonderful old man, Dr. John Yak, whose avocations after his retirement from medicine were botany and ornithology, approached me in the early seventies with a slim, hand-typed book ... Dr. Yak, then about 90, had catalogued each important specimen so that a comprehensive guide would be at the disposal of both the Park Board staff and the public.[2]

One day, when I was expressing my desire to know more about the ornamental trees growing in the Shakespeare and Perennial Garden, one of the gardeners gave me an out-of-circulation broadsheet publication titled *Trees of the Shakespeare Garden*. It provided the botanical information I needed for chapter 27. I wonder whether that circular partially relied on some of the work Dr. Yak had done.

Trees of the Shakespeare Garden was printed sometime after 1977, perhaps in the 1980s. How do I know? I tell the story in chapter 27. Solving such mysteries is like finding treasure—the tidbits that keep me researching.

"Trees and Shrubs of Stanley Park: English Bay to Lost Lagoon" is a chapter written by Don Benson and Alleyne Cook,[3] rhododendron experts, in *The Natural History of Stanley Park*.[4] The multi-paged list not only identifies hundreds of trees in Stanley Park but also locates them on a map. I was blessed to connect with and receive assistance from Alleyne and his wife, Barbara, in 2018. Alleyne Cook since died in his nineties in October 2019.

On November 11, 1988, Canada formally recognized Stanley Park as a National Historic Site.[5] It was the park's centennial year. Details of the park were captured in the Commemorative Integrity Statement for Stanley Park National Historic Site, prepared in November 2002 for the National Parks and National Historic Sites of Canada.[6] Of particular interest are the six pages of small print making up "Appendix 1: Ornamental Trees and Shrubs of Stanley Park (as Inventoried in the Areas West of Lost Lagoon in 1988)" by Benson and Cook.

"Ornamental Trees of Stanley Park" is the entry by Bill Stephen in *Wilderness on the Doorstep: Discovering Nature in Stanley Park*, a book written by Vancouver Natural History Society members and published by Harbour Publishing in June 2006. Bill Stephen was then an arborist technician with a forestry degree. His role before retiring in 2019 was Superintendent of Urban Forestry with the Vancouver Park Board. When I contacted Bill, almost at the completion of this book, he encouraged me to include any of the species he had listed in his "Ornamental Trees" article. I am grateful.

With a green canopy cover of 25.9 percent,[7] Vancouver is a city that inspires the world's arborists, urban foresters, and green-space planners and designers. In 2018, the first ever International Urban Forestry Congress was held in a hotel that looks out at Stanley Park. During the course of the four-day event, seven hundred congress participants attended nine field trips in Stanley Park, one each in the VanDusen Botanical Garden, Queen Elizabeth Park and the Bloedel Conservatory, the UBC Botanical Garden, and Dr. Sun Yat-Sen Classical Chinese Garden, and several other field trips in green spaces throughout the city. Five competitions in a Tree Climbing Championship—an aerial rescue, a belayed speed climb, an ascent event, a timed throwline event, and a work climb—were held in Stanley Park. This championship was hosted by the Pacific Northwest chapter of the International Society of Arboriculture.

This journey to learn more about the trees of Stanley Park has been a joy for me. I hope it is for you also.

I Am Grateful

I am incredibly grateful for the persistence, single-mindedness, and resolve of my fellow countryman Major James Skitt Matthews, the City of Vancouver's first archivist. I find it intriguing that Major Matthews was a Welshman who was seriously interested in Vancouver's history because I too was born in Wales and I've always been very interested in local Canadian history. I find it much more immediate and tangible than Welsh history.[8]

Major Matthews accomplished sterling work in archiving the personal history of Vancouver, a task that initially came without salary, space, formal training, or directives. I appreciate the very personal approach Major Matthews took in interviewing as many of Vancouver's pioneers as were willing to talk with him.

I thoroughly enjoyed reading Daphne Sleigh's scholarly work *The Man Who Saved Vancouver: Major James Skitt Matthews*. Sleigh breathes life into this irascible Welshman who insisted on single-handedly seeking out and detailing the early stories of Vancouver. With the early Vancouver stories came, of course, the Stanley Park stories.

The archives of the City of Vancouver came into being decades earlier than any other Canadian city's archives. Having been a collector all his life, when he reached his fifties, Major Matthews began what became Vancouver's city archives in 1929. In contrast, the City of Toronto Archives was formed in 1960, the City of Calgary Archives in 1981, and the City of Winnipeg first implemented a more careful Records Management Program (an archive) in 1996.

Once he was nominated as the city's archivist, in June 1931, Matthews never looked back and he never retired. Matthews died in office in 1970, and through the clever terms of his will, Vancouver City Council was led by the nose into building an actual City of Vancouver Archives, now occasionally known as "the Major Matthews." It is located at 1150 Chestnut Street, close to the Museum of Vancouver.

The City of Vancouver Archives curates a collection of irreplaceable historic photographs and maps that are easily accessible online.[9] These treasured early photographs were taken by Charles S. Bailey, William Bailey, Don Coltman, James Crookall, Fricke and Schenck, Howard King, Jack Lindsay, David Loughnan, W.J. Moore, Hamilton George Neelands, W.B. Shelly, Stephen J. Thompson, Stuart Thomson, Philip T. Timms, Richard Henry Trueman, Donn B.A. Williams, Warner Williams, and others.

I am grateful to fellow authors Dr. Ruth Derksen and Betsy Warland, one-off speakers at my Canadian Authors Association (CAA) monthly meetings. Each of them had messages that seemed to speak directly to me for writing this book. I am grateful to my circle of CAA writers, with whom I meet monthly. Your encouragement has been invaluable.

Without the thousands of hours put in by Vancouver Board of Parks and Recreation staff to assist Richard Steele in creating *The First 100 Years: The Vancouver Board of Parks and Recreation* (by "Mike R. Steele" on the book's cover), I would have been facing a huge amount of research time to find out about the multitude of decisions the Park Board made over the years. The many pages of entries in the chronology at the back of *The First 100 Years* made fascinating reading for me and gave me a timeline of Park Board history upon which I could pin other events, such as when specific trees were probably planted.

I thank Douglas Justice, adjunct professor at the School of Architecture + Landscape Architecture, at the University of British Columbia, for accepting me into his landscape architecture course in identifying trees and for providing me with permission to quote from his Vancouver Trees app. He and his colleagues Steven Clarke, Daniel Mosquin, and Karin England are the creators of this app, which is an essential resource for anyone interested in the trees growing by seed or by shovel in and around Vancouver.

I appreciate Canada's superb library system, an institution that we Canadians take for granted, but barely exists in other countries. Thank you for your tireless efforts to make old and new books available through both regular lending and interlibrary loans. Many were the times I borrowed Stanley Park–related books.

I have consulted Google Maps many times, for their ability to provide latitudes and longitudes, and for their satellite view of the park. When I run my mouse over an area of the park using Google Maps' satellite view, the tallest trees are quickly apparent—they seem to sway back and forth! In creating most of my early maps of tree locations, I used Google Maps combined with walking the terrain and checking the accuracy of my own draft maps.

I appreciate the community-authorship nature of Wikipedia, with its diligent checking of facts and its constant updating.

I am grateful to the generosity of family, friends, clients, and authors for writing and sharing their love of trees. Several of these appear as chapter epigraphs and more appear on my website, NinaShoroplova.ca.

I extend my hearty thanks to the following people:

- Rhododendron specialist Alleyne Cook and his wife, Barbara, who checked chapter 30, "Ted and Mary Greig Rhododendron Garden," for accuracy;

- Stacy Freeman, Vancouver Park Board gardener in the Shakespeare Garden;

- David Tracey, author of my first Stanley Park tree field guide, *Vancouver Tree Book*;

- Nature Vancouver and many of its members, including David Cook, Terry Taylor, and Stephen Partington;

- Stanley Park Ecology Society staff and volunteers, for their wonderful care of the park and for the walks they organize;

- My pre-Heritage House editor, Rebecca Coates, who polished up my manuscript in preparation for approaching a publisher.

Especially hearty thanks go to Bill Stephen, Vancouver Park Board's Superintendent of Urban Forestry at the time he wrote the foreword to this book. His generous words and his ongoing encouragement proved to be invaluable during my author journey. Early on in that journey, he helped me find even more specific trees in the park through the wonderful lists in his chapter "Ornamental Trees of Stanley Park" in *Wilderness on the Doorstep*. And later, he identified a couple of trees that were proving challenging. I will be forever grateful.

Heritage House created a magnificent team for me: Lara Kordic, editorial director; Marial Shea, structural and copy editor; and Jacqui Thomas, book and cover designer, and map maker; Grace Yaginuma, proofreader; and Martin Gavin, indexer. Thank you for generously sharing your brilliance for the benefit of this book. This has been a joyful journey of learning and listening to the wisdom of others. Thank you sincerely for sharing your many creative gifts.

Finally, I am grateful to my husband, Christian Shoroplov, for sometimes walking with me in the park, for insisting that the photos in this book be top quality, and for bearing with my absences while I was squirrelled away, learning to tell the difference between a vine maple and a bigleaf maple, a red oak and a pin oak, a Lawson cypress and a western redcedar, and a Douglas-fir and a western hemlock.

Appendix

List of the Legacy Trees

The trees that make up the *Legacy of Trees* in Stanley Park fall into four categories:

1. trees that are merely a memory and no longer around
2. trees with a plaque
3. trees that are special for some reason but without a plaque
4. trees and shrubs growing in the park and/or mentioned alphabetized by species

TREES THAT ARE MERELY A MEMORY AND NO LONGER AROUND

- Douglas-fir (*Pseudotsuga menziesii*) that became the first primitive crossing (chapter 5)
- Douglas-fir that stood sentinel at the Georgia Street entrance to the park until around 1918 (chapter 7)
- Monkey puzzle trees (*Araucaria araucana*) that used to be behind the Oppenheimer bust (chapter 15) and beside the Robert Burns statue (chapter 32)
- Western white pine (*Pinus monticola*) that used to be in the Shakespeare Garden (chapter 27)
- English holly (*Ilex aquifolium*) trees that used to be near the Robert Burns statue (chapter 32)
- Skeleton tree beloved by crows in the Second Beach swimming pool enclosure

TREES WITH A PLAQUE

- Ancient western redcedar (*Thuja plicata*) known as the Hollow Tree (chapter 9)
- Sydney A. Pascall Japanese cedar (*Cryptomeria japonica* 'Lobbii') (chapter 16)
- English oak (*Quercus robur*) planted by Mrs. Jonathan Rogers for the tercentenary of Shakespeare's death (chapter 17)
- "Comedy" English oak (*Quercus robur*)
- "Tragedy" English oak (*Quercus robur*)
- Drainie Pacific dogwood (*Cornus nuttallii*)
- Queen Elizabeth Windsor oak (*Quercus robur*) (chapter 23)
- P.Z. Caverhill Douglas-fir (*Pseudotsuga menziesii*) (chapter 25)
- Junior Forest Wardens Douglas-fir (*Pseudotsuga menziesii*)
- Frances Elizabeth Willard white camellia (*Camellia*)
- Western redcedar (*Thuja plicata*) (chapter 27, "Shakespeare Garden Trees")
- Western hemlock (*Tsuga heterophylla*)
- Red oak (*Quercus rubra*)
- Black locust (*Robinia pseudoacacia*)
- Black walnut (*Juglans nigra*)
- Atlas cedar (*Cedrus atlantica*)
- Powys Thomas red oak (*Quercus rubra*)
- Grove of daybreak cherries (*Prunus × yedoensis*)
- Silver birch, a.k.a. European white birch (*Betula pendula*), known as the Peace Train tree (chapter 31)
- Western redcedar (*Thuja plicata*) known as the 125th anniversary tree at Chaythoos (chapter 33)

TREES THAT ARE SPECIAL FOR SOME REASON BUT WITHOUT A PLAQUE

- Western redcedar (*Thuja plicata*) with half a dozen stories to tell (chapters 5, 17, and 18)
- Western redcedar (*Thuja plicata*) that became known as the *National Geographic* tree, now fallen and providing nourishment to the flora around it (chapter 10)

A Persian silk tree
(*Albizia julibrissin*).

- Stump known as the two-spirit carving (chapter 10)
- Tree that grows on top of Siwash Rock (chapter 11)
- Western redcedar (*Thuja plicata*) that is the one remaining Sister of the Seven Sisters (chapter 12)
- Martha Smith's lilac bushes (*Syringa vulgaris*) (chapter 13)
- English oak (*Quercus robur*) beside Brockton Oval planted for the coronation of King Edward VII (chapter 14)
- Red alder (*Alnus rubra*) that overlooks Third Beach and once held a record for being the second-largest red alder in Canada (chapter 19)
- London plane trees (*Platanus × hispanica*) growing in a curved avenue (chapter 21)
- Ornamental flowering cherry sentinel tree, a *Prunus* Sato Zakura Group 'Ojochin' (chapter 22)
- Jody Taylor bigleaf maple (*Acer macrophyllum*) (chapter 23)
- Avenue and triangle of horse chestnut trees and one shagbark hickory (*Carya ovata*)
- The heronry trees, which are mostly horse chestnuts (*Aesculus*), some maples (*Acer*), English oaks (*Quercus robur*), and London plane trees (*Platanus × hispanica*)
- Debarked catalpa that fell in the windstorm of 2006 (chapter 24)
- Douglas-fir (*Pseudotsuga menziesii*) with an eagle's nest in Salmon Stream Valley (chapter 25)
- Western redcedar (*Thuja plicata*) at the Vancouver Aquarium
- Blue Atlas cedar tree (*Cedrus atlantica* 'Glauca') espaliered against the front wall of the Vancouver Park Board offices (chapter 29)
- London plane tree at the Air India memorial (chapter 31)
- Three dove trees (*Davidia involucrata*), a.k.a. pocket handkerchief trees, at the Air India memorial
- Young English oak (*Quercus robur*) that takes the place of the English oak from Windsor Great Park that was planted in 1937 for Lord Stanley (chapter 33)

TREES AND SHRUBS GROWING IN
THE PARK AND/OR MENTIONED

NOTE: Invasive plants are not listed here.

- *Abies grandis*—grand fir
- *Acer*—maple
  - *A. campestre*—field maple
  - *A. circinatum*—vine maple
  - *A. davidii* subsp. *davidii*—snake bark maple
  - *A. douglasii*—Douglas maple
  - *A. griseum*—paperbark maple
  - *A. japonicum*—ornamental maple
  - *A. macrophyllum*—bigleaf maple
  - *A. negundo*—box elder, a.k.a. Manitoba maple
  - *A. palmatum*—common Japanese maple
  - *A. palmatum var. dissectum*—splitleaf maple
  - *A. platanoides*—Norway maple
  - *A. platanoides* 'Crimson King'—Crimson King Norway maple
  - *A. pseudoplatanus* 'Leopoldii'—variegated sycamore maple
  - *A. saccharinum*—silver maple
  - *A. saccharum* subsp. *grandidentatum*—big tooth maple
  - *A. shirasawanum*—full moon maple, a.k.a. shirasawa maple

- *Aesculus*—buckeye and horse chestnut
    - *A. hippocastanum*—white horse chestnut
    - *A. pavia*—red buckeye, a.k.a. red horse chestnut
    - *A.* × *carnea* 'Briotii'—ruby red horse chestnut
- *Ailanthus altissima*—tree of heaven
- *Albizia julibrissin*—Persian silk tree , a.k.a. pink silk tree and mimosa
- *Alnus rubra*—red alder
- *Araucaria araucana*—monkey puzzle tree
- *Arbutus menziesii*—arbutus, a.k.a. Pacific madrone
- *Berberis*—barberry
    - *B. aquifolium* (used to be known as *Mahonia aquifolium*)—Oregon grape
    - *B.* × *hortensis*—also commonly called Oregon grape
- *Betula*—birch
    - *B. albosinensis* var. *septentrionalis*—Chinese red-bark birch
    - *B. papyrifera*—paper birch
    - *B. pendula*—European white birch , a.k.a. silver birch
    - *B. pendula* 'Dalecarlica'—cut-leaf birch, a.k.a. Swedish birch
- *Buddleja*—butterfly bush , a.k.a. buddleia
    - *B. alternifolia*—alternate-leaved butterfly bush , a.k.a. buddleia
    - *B. globosa*—orange ball buddleia, a.k.a. orange-ball-tree
- *Callicarpa bodinieri giraldii*—beautyberry
- *Calocedrus decurrens*—incense cedar
- *Camellia*—camellia
    - *C. sinensis*—tea plant
    - *C.* × *williamsii* 'Donation'—donation camellia

Oregon grape (*Berberis aquifolium*) begins to flower in March.

- *Carya ovata*—shagbark hickory
- *Castanea sativa*—sweet chestnut
- *Catalpa*
    - *C. bignonioides*—southern catalpa
    - *C. speciosa*—northern catalpa
- *Cedrus*—cedar
    - *C. atlantica*—Atlas cedar
    - *C. atlantica* 'Glauca'—blue atlas cedar
    - *C. deodara*—Himalayan cedar, a.k.a. deodar cedar
- *Cercidiphyllum japonicum*—katsura
- *Chamaecyparis*—false cypress
    - *C. lawsoniana*—Lawson cypress
    - *C. lawsoniana* 'Stewartii'—*golden Lawson cypress*
    - *C. lawsoniana* 'Wisselii'—*Wisselii Lawson cypress*
    - *C. nootkatensis*, a.k.a. *Cupressus nootkatensis*— Nootka cypress, a.k.a. yellow cedar
    - *C. pisifera* 'Filifera'—Sawara false cypress
    - *C. pisifera* 'Plumosa'—plumose Sawara false cypress

- *C. pisifera* 'Squarrosa'—Sawara false cypress
  - × *Chitalpa tashkentensis*—catalpa × desert willow
- *Clerodendrum trichotomum*—harlequin glorybower
- *Cornus*—dogwood
  - *C. alternifolia* 'Argentea'—variegated pagoda dogwood
  - *C. controversa*—giant dogwood
  - *C. florida*—eastern dogwood
  - *C. florida* × *C. nuttallii*—Eddie's White Wonder dogwood
  - *C. florida* 'Rubra'—pink-flowering dogwood
  - *C. florida* × *C. nuttallii*—Eddie's White Wonder dogwood
  - *C. kousa*—kousa dogwood
  - *C. nuttallii*—Pacific dogwood
  - *C. nuttallii* 'Goldspot'—Pacific dogwood
- *Corylopsis sinensis*—Chinese winter hazel
- *Corylus*—hazelnut
  - *C. avellana*—European hazelnut
  - *C. avellana* 'Contorta'—Harry Lauder's walking stick
  - *C. avellana* 'Purpurea'—purple hazelnut
- *Cotoneaster salicifolius*—willow-leaved cotoneaster
- *Crataegus laevigata*—English hawthorn
- *Cryptomeria japonica* 'Lobbii'—Japanese false cedar, a.k.a. sugi
- *Cunninghamia lanceolata*—China fir
- *Cupressus nootkatensis*, a.k.a. *Chamaecyparis nootkatensis*—Nootka cypress, a.k.a. yellow cedar
- *Daphne mezereum*—February daphne
- *Davidia involucrata*—dove tree , a.k.a. handkerchief tree, pocket handkerchief tree, and ghost tree

- *Decaisnea fargesii*—dead man's fingers , a.k.a. blue bean plant and blue sausage fruit
- *Enkianthus campanulatus*—redvein enkianthus
- *Eucalyptus*—gum tree
- *Fagus*—beech
  - *F. sylvatica*—European beech
  - *F. sylvatica* 'Aspleniifolia'—fernleaf beech
  - *F. sylvatica* 'Dawyck'—Dawyck beech
  - *F. sylvatica* 'Pendula'—weeping beech
  - *F. sylvatica* 'Rohanii'—Rohani beech
  - *F. sylvatica* 'Roseomarginata'—tricolour beech, a.k.a. pink nightie beech
  - *F. sylvatica purpurea*—copper beech
- *Ficus*—fig tree
- *Fraxinus*—ash
  - *F. excelsior*—European ash
  - *F. ornus*—manna ash, a.k.a. flowering ash
  - *F. ornus* 'Arie Peters'—Arie Peters manna ash
- *Garrya elliptica*—silk tassel bush
- *Ginkgo biloba*—maidenhair tree
- *Gymnocladus dioicus*—Kentucky coffeetree
- *Hamamelis*—witch hazel
  - *H. mollis*—Chinese witch hazel
  - *H. virgiana*—witch hazel
- *Ilex aquifolium*—English holly
- *Juglans*—walnut
  - *J. nigra*—black walnut
  - *J. regia*—English walnut
- *Kalmia latifolia*—mountain laurel, a.k.a. calico-bush and spoonwood
- *Koelreuteria paniculata*—golden raintree
- *Laburnum anagyroides*—golden chain tree, a.k.a. common laburnum and golden rain
- *Larix occidentalis*—western larch

- *Liquidambar styraciflua*—sweetgum
- *Liriodendron tulipifera*—tulip tree, a.k.a. yellow poplar
- *Magnolia*—magnolia
  - *M.* 'Yellow Lantern,' a.k.a. *M. acuminata* var. *subcordata* × *M.* × *soulangeana* '*Alexandrina*'—yellow lantern magnolia
  - *M. acuminata* × *M. denudata* 'Butterflies'
  - *M. dawsoniana*—Dawson's magnolia
  - *M. dawsoniana* 'Barbara Cook'—Barbara Cook magnolia
  - *M. grandiflora*—southern magnolia
  - *M. hypoleuca*—Japanese cucumber tree
  - *M. kobus*—kobus magnolia
  - *M. sieboldii*—Siebold's magnolia , a.k.a. Korean mountain magnolia and Oyama magnolia
  - *M. stellata*—star magnolia
  - *M. tripetala*—umbrella tree
  - *M. virginiana*—sweetbay magnolia
  - *M. wilsonii*—Wilson's magnolia
  - *M.* × *soulangeana*—saucer magnolia
- *Malus fusca*—Pacific crabapple
- *Metasequoia glyptostroboides*—dawn redwood
- *Nothofagus antarctica*—Antarctic beech
- *Notholithocarpus densiflorus*—tanoak, a.k.a. tanbark oak
- *Nyssa*—tupelo
  - *N. sylvatica*—black tupelo
  - *N. sylvatica* 'Pendula'—weeping black tupelo
- *Osmanthus delavayi*—Delavay tea olive
- *Paulownia tomentosa*—princess tree , a.k.a. foxglove tree
- *Phellodendron amurense*—Amur cork tree
- *Photinia serrulata*—Chinese photinia

Looking up into the crown of a Douglas-fir.

- *Picea*—spruce
  - *P. abies*—Norway spruce
  - *P. omorika*—Serbian spruce
  - *P. pungens*—Colorado blue spruce
  - *P. pungens* 'Glauca'—Colorado blue spruce
  - *P. sitchensis*—Sitka spruce
- *Pinus*—pine
  - *P. contorta*—shore pine
  - *P. jeffreyi*—Jeffrey pine, a.k.a. yellow pine
  - *P. monticola*—western white pine
  - *P. mugo*—mugo pine
  - *P. nigra*—black pine
  - *P. nigra* subsp. *laricio*—Austrian black pine, a.k.a. Corsican pine
  - *P. parviflora*—Japanese white pine
  - *P. ponderosa*—ponderosa pine, a.k.a. bull pine, blackjack pine, and western yellow-pine

- *P. sylvestris* 'Fastigiata'—upright Scots pine
- *P. wallichiana*—Himalayan white pine
- *Platanus*—plane tree
  - *P.* × *hispanica*—London plane tree
  - *P.* × *hispanica* 'Bloodgood'—London plane tree
  - *P. occidentalis*—American sycamore
- *Populus trichocarpa*—northern black cottonwood
- *Prunus*— a genus that includes flowering and fruiting almonds, apricots, cherries, nectarines, peaches, and plums
  - *P. emarginata*—wild bitter cherry tree
  - *P. lusitanica*—Portuguese laurel
  - *P. sargentii* 'Rancho'—rancho cherry
  - *P.* Sato Zakura Group 'Gyoiko'—Gyoiko flowering cherry; 'Ojochin'—Ojochin flowering cherry; 'Shirotae'—Shirotae flowering cherry; 'Shujaku'—Shujaku flowering cherry
  - *P. serrulata* 'Snow Goose'—Snow Goose flowering cherry
  - *P. serrulata* 'Ukon'—Ukon flowering cherry
  - *P.* × *subhirtella* 'Atsumori'—Atsumori double flowering cherry
  - *P.* × *subhirtella* 'Autumnalis Rosea'—Autumnalis Rosea winter-flowering cherry
  - *P.* × *yedoensis*—daybreak cherry
- *Pseudotsuga menziesii*—Douglas-fir
- *Quercus*—oak
  - *Q. coccinea*—scarlet oak
  - *Q. frainetto* 'Forest Green'—Hungarian oak
  - *Q. palustris*—pin oak
  - *Q. rubra*—red oak
  - *Q. robur*—English oak

- *Q. turneri*, a.k.a. *Q. ilex* × *Q. robur*—Turner's oak
- *Rhamnus purshiana*—cascara
- *Rhododendron*—rhododendrons and azaleas
  - *R.* 'Aladdin'
  - *R.* 'Anna Rose Whitney'
  - *R.* 'Azor'
  - *R.* 'Baden Baden'
  - *R.* 'Beauty of Littleworth'
  - *R.* 'Beethoven'
  - *R.* 'Bonfire'
  - *R.* 'Chionoides'
  - *R.* 'Cilpinense'
  - *R.* 'Crest'
  - *R.* 'Cunningham's White'
  - *R.* 'Electra'
  - *R.* 'Elizabeth'
  - *R.* 'Fabia'
  - *R.* 'Fastuosum Flore Pleno'
  - *R.* 'George Watling'
  - *R.* 'Haydn'
  - *R.* 'Impi'
  - *R.* 'Lady Clementine Mitford'
  - *R.* 'May Day'
  - *R.* 'Moonstone'
  - *R.* 'Mrs. A.T. de la Mare'
  - *R.* 'Mrs. Furnival'
  - *R.* 'Naomi Hope'
  - *R.* 'Naomi Nautilus'
  - *R.* 'Palestrina'
  - *R.* 'Point Defiance'
  - *R.* 'President Roosevelt'
  - *R.* 'Purple Splendor'
  - *R.* 'Royston Red'

- R. 'Sappho'
- R. 'Scintillation'
- R. 'Susan'
- R. 'The Honourable Jean Marie de Montague'
- R. 'Unique'
- R. 'Wedding Present'
- R. 'Whitney's Orange'
- R. 'Yellow Hammer'
- *R. ambiguum*
- *R. arboreum*
- *R. atlanticum*
- *R. augustinii*
- *R. auriculatum*
- *R. cinnabarinum* x
- *R. decorum*
- *R. fortunei* x
- *R. occidentale*
- *R. schlippenbachii*
- *R. smirnowii*
- *Rhus*—sumac
- *Robinia pseudoacacia*—black locust
  - *R. pseudoacacia* 'Frisia'—golden locust
- *Salix*—willow
  - *S.* 'Chrysocoma'—weeping willow·
  - *S. matsudana* 'Tortuosa'—corkscrew willow
- *Sambucus racemosa*—elderberry
- *Sciadopitys verticillata*—umbrella pine
- *Sequoia sempervirens*—coast redwood, a.k.a. California redwood
- *Sequoiadendron giganteum*—giant sequoia, a.k.a. Sierra redwood
- *Sophora japonica*, a.k.a. *Styphnolobium japonicum*—Japanese pagoda tree, a.k.a. scholar tree

- *Sorbus*—mountain ash
  - *S. aucuparia*—European mountain ash
  - *S. vilmorinii*—Vilmorin's rowan
- *Stachyurus praecox*—early spiketail
- *Stewartia pseudocamellia*—Japanese stuartia
- *Styphnolobium japonicum*, a.k.a. *Sophora japonica*—Japanese pagoda tree , a.k.a. scholar tree
- *Styrax*—snowbell
  - *S. japonicus*—Japanese snowbell
  - *S. obassia*—fragrant snowbell
- *Syringa vulgaris*—lilac
- *Taxodium distichum*—baldcypress
- *Taxus*—yew
  - *T. baccata* 'Dovastoniana' or *T. cuspidata* 'Intermedia'—either a Westfelton yew or a Japanese yew
  - *T. brevifolia*—Pacific yew
- *Thuja*—cedar
  - *T. plicata*—western redcedar
  - *T. plicata* 'Zebrina'—variegated western redcedar
- *Tilia*—linden tree
  - *T. cordata*—little-leaf linden
  - *T. platyphyllos*—large-leaf linden
- *Trochodendron aralioides*—wheel tree
- *Tsuga*—hemlock
  - *T. heterophylla*—western hemlock
  - *T. mertensiana*—mountain hemlock
- *Ulmus minor* 'Sarniensis'—English elm
- *Umbellularia californica*—California laurel
- *Viburnum*—viburnum
  - *V. carlesii*—Korean-spice viburnum
  - *V. plicatum* 'Lanarth'—Lanarth viburnum , a.k.a. Japanese snowball

Notes

INTRODUCTION

1. Vancouver Board of Park Commissioners, *Map of Stanley Park, Vancouver, B.C.*, 1911, City of Vancouver Archives, searcharchives.vancouver.ca/map-of-stanley-park-vancouver-b-c.

2. A trail map of Stanley Park is available at vancouver.ca/files/cov/Stanley-Park-trails-map.pdf. Find printable maps at vancouver.ca/parks-recreation-culture/printable-map-of-stanley-park.aspx.

3. I've created a page for *Legacy of Trees* at ninashoroplova.ca/wp/home/my-books/legacy-of-trees.

CHAPTER 1

1. Matthews, *Early Vancouver*, 1:52. See the image of the first train to arrive in Vancouver, on Dominion Day, May 23, 1887. Note the decorations for Queen Victoria's Jubilee, the fiftieth year of her reign.

2. "Excerpt from Minutes in Original Minute Book of Proceedings of First City Council at its Second Meeting, 12 May 1886, at 7.30 PM," in Matthews, *Early Vancouver*, 3:190. Also see Manitoba Historical Society's entry on Arthur Wellington Ross at "Memorable Manitobans: Arthur Wellington Ross (1846-1901)," Manitoba Historical Society, last modified December 2, 2018, mhs.mb.ca/docs/people/ross_aw.shtml.

3. "First Meeting of Council—May 10, 1886," Transcribimus, transcribed in 2012, transcribimus.ca/may-10-1886/.

4. "Vancouver Wants Coal Harbour Peninsula for a Public Park—May 12, 1886," Transcribimus, transcribed in 2012, transcribimus.ca/may-12-1886/.

5. Matthews, *Early Vancouver*, 1:208. A floor plan of the "Swearing In" of the First City Council.

6. "Council Endorses Lower Qualifications for Voters, Elected Officials—February 27, 1888," Transcribimus, transcribed in 2014, transcribimus.ca/feb-27-1888/.

7. *The Canadian Encyclopedia*, s.v. "Charles Hill-Tout," thecanadianencyclopedia.ca/en/article/charles-hill-tout/.

8. Steele, *First 100 Years*, 201.

9. Matthews, *Early Vancouver*, 4:66.

10 "Stanley Park National Historic Site of Canada," Parks Canada Directory of Federal Heritage Designations, pc.gc.ca/apps/dfhd/page_nhs_eng.aspx?id=84.

11 TripAdvisor, "TripAdvisor Announces World's Top Landmarks and Parks in Travelers' Choice Attractions Awards," news release, June 17, 2014, ir.tripadvisor.com/news-releases/news-release-details/tripadvisor-announces-worlds-top-landmarks-and-parks-travelers.

CHAPTER 3

1. Parish and Thomson, *Tree Book*.

2. Terry Taylor, "Trees of Stanley Park," in *Wilderness on the Doorstep*, ed. Parkinson. Used with permission of Terry Taylor.

3. Steele, *First 100 Years*, 229.

CHAPTER 4

1. Matthews, Early Vancouver, 2:57. This is according to an interview between Major Matthews and Qoitchetahl (Andrew Paul), the secretary of the Squamish Indian Council from 1911 and still serving in that position in 1933 (at the time of the interview).

2. Matthews, *Early Vancouver*, 6:109–12. This is according to an interview between Major Matthews and August Jack Khahtsahlano.

3. Matthews, *Early Vancouver*, 7:128. The interview was held on July 14, 1951.

CHAPTER 5

1. Vancouver, *Voyage of Discovery*, 1:xv.

2. Menzies, *Menzies' Journal*, 89–90. Entry from July 21, 1792, while on the north end of Vancouver Island. Bracketed text appeared in the margins of the original journal.

3. McCarthy, *Monkey Puzzle Man*.

4. Davies, *Douglas of the Forests*, 175. Also see Douglas, *Journal Kept by David Douglas*, 340.

5. F.A.S., "*Pseudotsuga menziesii* versus *Pseudotsuga taxifolia*," *Taxon* 5, no. 2 (April 1956): 38–39, iapt-taxon.org/historic/ Congress/IBC_1959/pseudots_men02.pdf.

6. Searchable versions of Matthews's *Early Vancouver* are available online at former. vancouver.ca/ctyclerk/archives/digitized/ EarlyVan/index.htm and vancouver.ca/ your-government/major-matthews-early- vancouver.aspx.

7. Matthews, *Early Vancouver*, 2:210–11. "Manuscript written by Mrs. Emily Eldon, 1150 Alberni Street, at request [of] Major Matthews following conversation at Pioneers Picnic, Newcastle Island, June 15, 1932."

8. The photo is from the City of Vancouver Archives website at searcharchives.vancouver. ca/stanley-park-with-mr-elder-park-super- intendent-and-his-wife-in-front-of-their- cottage-at-entrance-to-stanley-park. In the description of this photograph, their surname Eldon is misspelled as "Elder."

9. Steele, *First 100 Years*, 212.

CHAPTER 6

Chapter epigraph from "City Debentures to Be Sold to Finance Fire Engine—June 22, 1886," Transcribimus, transcribed in 2012, transcribimus.ca/jun-22-1886/.

CHAPTER 7

1. Steele, *First 100 Years*, 213.

2. Johnson, "Deadman's Island" in *Legends of Vancouver*.

3. Tracey, *Vancouver Tree Book*, 67. Used with permission.

4. Steele, *First 100 Years*, 220 (my italics).

CHAPTER 8

1. Andy Coghlan, "Trees May Have a 'Heartbeat' That Is So Slow We Never Noticed It," *New Scientist*, April 20, 2018, newscientist.com/ article/2167003-trees-may-have-a-heartbeat- that-is-so-slow-we-never-noticed-it/.

2. Andy Coghlan, "Trees Seen Resting Branches While 'Asleep' for the First Time," *New Scientist*, May 18, 2016, newscientist.com/ article/2088833-trees-seen-resting-branches- while-asleep-for-the-first-time/.

CHAPTER 9

1. See the photo on online at en.wikipedia. org/wiki/Hollow_Tree#/media/ File:A_big_visitor_to_the_big_tree_in_ Stanley_Park,_Vancouver_B.C..jpg.

2. "10. Hollow Tree (Stanley Park) [saved]," 2009 Top10 Watch List, Heritage Vancouver, heritagevancouver.org/top10-watch- list/2009/10-hollow-tree-stanley-park/.

3. Karen Wonders, *Conservation Plan for Stanley Park's Hollow Tree* (Vancouver, BC: Stanley Park Hollow Tree Conservation Society), cathedral- grove.eu/media/01-4-conservation.pdf.

4. "Golden Tree," Douglas Coupland (website), coupland.com/public-arts/golden-tree.

CHAPTER 10

Chapter epigraph from Ira Sutherland, "The Stanley Park Forest," Vancouver Big Tree Hiking Guide, vancouversbigtrees.com. Used with permission.

1. These websites include Vancouver Big Tree Hiking Guide (vancouversbigtrees.com) and Monumental Trees (monumentaltrees.com/en/can/). See also Uliya Talmazan, "Canada's Second Largest Douglas Fir Tree May Have Been Found Near Port Renfrew, *Global News*, March 27, 2014, globalnews.ca/news/1235236/canadas-second-largest-Douglas-fir-tree-may-have-been-found-near-port-renfrew/.

2. Gregg Koep, "Stanley Park's National Geographic Tree," February 23, 2013, Vancouver Island Big Trees, vancouverislandbigtrees.blogspot.com/2013/02/stanley-parks-national-geographic-tree.html.

3. "Two Spirits Artwork," StanleyParkVan.com, stanleyparkvan.com/stanley-park-van-art-two-spirits.html.

4. *First Peoples: A Guide for Newcomers* (Vancouver, BC: City of Vancouver, 2014), vancouver.ca/files/cov/First-Peoples-A-Guide-for-Newcomers.pdf.

CHAPTER 11

1. Major James Skitt Matthews, *Woman Sitting on Rock Formation Known as Siwash Rock's Wife, Sketching*, 189-?, silver gelatin print, 8.5 × 11 cm, City of Vancouver Archives, searcharchives.vancouver.ca/woman-sitting-on-rock-formation-known-as-siwash-rocks-wife-sketching.

2. Matthews, *Early Vancouver*, 4:204. For a photo of Sunz Rock, see Major James Skitt Matthews, *Sunz Rock at Prospect Point*, silver gelatin print, 15 × 12 cm, City of Vancouver Archives, searcharchives.vancouver.ca/sunz-rock-at-prospect-point;rad.

3. Johnson, "The Siwash Rock," in *Legends of Vancouver*.

4. Ibid.

CHAPTER 12

1. Johnson, "The Lure in Stanley Park," in *Legends of Vancouver*.

CHAPTER 13

1. Barman, *Stanley Park's Secret*. I am indebted to Jean Barman for the excellent way she chronicles the lives of Martha and Peter Smith and their Stanley Park neighbours. This chapter relies on Barman's book.

CHAPTER 14

Chapter epigraph quoted in Matthews, *Early Vancouver*, 4:260.

1. Matthews, *Early Vancouver*, 1:141. Major Matthews interviewed Justice Beck in 1931.

2. Ibid.

3. Steele, *First 100 Years*, 211.

4. Chuck Davis, "Vancouver's Nine O'Clock Gun," The History of Metropolitan Vancouver, vancouverhistory.ca/archives_gun.htm.

5. Matthews, *Early Vancouver*, 4:260.

6. Brockton Pavilion's website is brocktonpavilion.ca.

CHAPTER 15

1 "David Oppenheimer," Public Art Registry, City of Vancouver, covapp.vancouver.ca/PublicArtRegistry/ArtworkDetail.aspx?ArtworkId=103.

2 Ibid.

CHAPTER 16

1 "Friendship Trees in the Harris Study," Rotary Global History Fellowship, rghfhome.org/first100/presidents/1910harris/paulharris/office/trees.htm.

2. Wikipedia, s.v. "Cryptomeria," en.wikipedia.org/wiki/Cryptomeria.

3. "Harding Memorial Sculpture," Public Art Registry, City of Vancouver, covapp.vancouver.ca/PublicArtRegistry/ArtworkDetail.aspx?FromArtworkSearch=True&ArtworkId=87.

CHAPTER 17

1. "Vancouver Shakespeare Society," City of Vancouver Archives, searcharchives.vancouver.ca/vancouver-shakespeare-society.

2. For those interested in reading the play written in 1913, the text is available online. Henry V. Esmond, *Eliza Comes to Stay: A Farce in Three Acts* (New York: Samuel French, 1913), catalog. hathitrust.org/Record/009585226.

3. IMDb (Internet Movie Database), s.v. "John Martin Harvey," imdb.com/name/nm0367590/bio. Used with permission.

4. Ibid.

5. Ibid.

6. Denis Salter, review of Living the Part: John Drainie and the Dilemma of Canadian Stardom, by Bronwyn Drainie, *Theatre History Studies* 9 (January 1, 1989): 173.

7. "ACTRA's John Drainie Award," ACTRA Awards, ACTRA (Alliance of Canadian Cinema, Television and Radio Artists), actra.ca/media-centre/actra-awards/.

8. Wikipedia, s.v. "Drainie-Taylor Biography Prize," en.wikipedia.org/wiki/Drainie-Taylor_Biography_Prize.

CHAPTER 18

1 Johnson, "Deadman's Island," in *Legends of Vancouver.*

CHAPTER 20

Chapter epigraph from Gerald B. Straley, *Trees of Vancouver* (page xiii) © UBC Press, 1992. Reprinted with permission. All rights reserved by the publisher.

1. *Oak Tree: Nature's Greatest Survivor*, directed by Nic Stacey, presented by George McGavin, aired March 11, 2019, on BBC4, bbc.co.uk/programmes/b06fq03t.

2. *Scientific American*, "How Do Large Trees, Such as Redwoods, Get Water from Their Roots to the Leaves?," February 8, 1999, scientificamerican.com/article/how-do-large-trees-such-a/.

CHAPTER 21

1. For example, the photo *H.R.H. Duke of Connaught's Visit to Vancouver, Sept. 1912* (Open Collections, University of British Columbia library, open.library.ubc.ca/collections/langmann/items/1.0361069) was previously titled *Portrait of the Duke and Duchess of Connaught at the Civic Reception Held for Their Visit at the Vancouver Court House. Mayor James Findlay Can Be Seen behind the Duke.* I informed UBC archivists on June 14, 2018, that this photograph is not of the Vancouver Court House (as previously identified) but the Brockton Oval Grandstand, as seen by the construction style of the stand visible above the crowd.

2. John Mackie, "This Week in History: 1947 Lumbermen's Arch Is Demolished," *Vancouver Sun*, December 2, 2016, vancouversun.com/news/local-news/this-week-in-history-1947-lumbermens-arch-is-demolished.

3. To see archival images of these arches, go to the City of Vancouver Archives website at searcharchives.vancouver.ca. Do an advanced search using Boolean search terms.

4. Chuck Davis, "1919," The History of Metropolitan Vancouver, vancouverhistory.ca/chronology1919.htm.

CHAPTER 22

1. *Canadian Japanese Society at Japanese Memorial in Stanley Park*, black and white nitrate negative, 10 × 12 cm, item CVA 99-2644, City of Vancouver Archives, searcharchives.vancouver.ca/canadian-japanese-society-at-japanese-memorial-in-stanley-park.

2. *The Canadian Encyclopedia*, s.v. "Internment of Japanese Canadians," the-canadianencyclopedia.ca/en/article/internment-of-japanese-canadians/. Used with permission.

3. *Return: A Commemorative Yearbook in Honour of the Japanese Canadian Students of 1942* (Vancouver, BC: The Ubyssey, 2012), issuu.com/ubyssey/docs/2_returns_yearbook_ubc/69.

4. Ibid.

CHAPTER 23

1. Bill Stephen, "Ornamental Trees of Stanley Park," in *Wilderness on the Doorstep*, ed. Parkinson.

2. Tracey, *Vancouver Tree Book*, 6.

3. "Fund for Tristen Taylor," created April 1, 2016, GoFundMe, gofundme.com/czx35wt8.

4. Matthews, *Early Vancouver*, 4:203.

5. "Townley, Alice Ashworth," Digitized Collections, Simon Fraser University library, digital.lib.sfu.ca/ceww-908/townley-alice-ashworth.

6. "Vancouver's Great Blue Herons," Urban Wildlife, Stanley Park Ecology Society, stanleyparkecology.ca/conservation/urban-wildlife/herons/.

7. "Watch the Pacific Great Blue Herons Live from Stanley Park," Parks, Recreation, and Culture, City of Vancouver, vancouver.ca/parks-recreation-culture/heron-cam.aspx.

CHAPTER 24

Chapter epigraph from Matthews, *Early Vancouver*, 6:119.

1. BC History, "1938 Colour Film Footage of the Construction of the Lion's Gate Bridge," YouTube video, youtube.com/watch?v=HYNAoDlNN9Q.

2. Stanley Park Ecology Society, *Stanley Park Ecology Society Guide to Invasive Plant Management in Stanley Park* (Vancouver, BC: Stanley Park Ecology Society), stanleyparkecology.ca/wp-content/uploads/downloads/2012/02/SOPEI-Invasive-plant-BMPs-for-Stanley-Park.pdf.

CHAPTER 25

1. For a closer look, see Vancouver Board of Park Commissioners, *Map of Stanley Park, Vancouver, B.C.*, 1911, City of Vancouver Archives, searcharchives.vancouver.ca/map-of-stanley-park-vancouver-b-c.

2. "Restoring a Species," The American Chestnut Foundation, acf.org/the-american-chestnut/restoring-a-species/.

3. "Eagles Nesting in Stanley Park," February 28th, 2018, Stanley Park Ecology Society, stanleyparkecology.ca/2018/02/28/eagles-nesting-stanley-park/.

4. The Nauticapedia, s.v. "Ship Details: P.Z. Caverhill," nauticapedia.ca/dbase/Query/Shiplist4.php?&name=P.Z.%20Caverhill&id=12969.

5. Steele, *First 100 Years*, 237.

6. There are two misspellings on this plaque: *Francis* should be *Frances* and *Woman's* should be *Women's*.

7. "Biography," Frances Willard House Museum and Archives, franceswillardhouse.org/frances-willard/biography/.

8. *Frances E. Willard—Founder of the World's Women's Christian Temperance Union* (Vancouver, BC: Heritage Vancouver Society, 2014), heritagevancouver.org/pdf_articles/Heritage-Vancouver-event-Frances-Willard.pdf.

9. Stevie Wilson, "The Stanley Park Zoo: A Vancouver Institution until 1996," *Scout Magazine*, December 4, 2014, scoutmagazine.ca/2014/12/04/you-should-know-more-about-the-stanley-park-zoo-a-vancouver-institution-until-1996/.

CHAPTER 26

Chapter epigraph from Alice Huang, "Totem Poles," Indigenous Foundations, indigenous-foundations.arts.ubc.ca/totem_poles/.

1. Ibid.

2. Ibid.

3. Chuck Davis, "1912," The History of Metropolitan Vancouver, vancouverhistory. ca/chronology9.htm.

4. Chuck Davis, "1936," The History of Metropolitan Vancouver, vancouverhistory. ca/chronology1936.htm.

5. "Thunderbird Dynasty Poll, 1936," *Vancouver Is Awesome*, February 26, 2017, vancouverisawesome.com/history/ thunderbird-dynasty-pole-1936-1933440.

6. "First Nations Art and Totem Poles: 'People Amongst the People' Coast Salish Gateways," Parks, Recreation, and Culture, City of Vancouver, vancouver.ca/parks-recreation-culture/totems-and-first-nations-art.aspx.

7. "Symbols of the City of Vancouver," City of Vancouver, vancouver.ca/news-calendar/ city-symbols.aspx.

CHAPTER 27

1. "Shakespeare Garden," Places That Matter Community History Resource (Vancouver Heritage Foundation), vancouverheritagefoundation.org/place-that-matters/ shakespeare-garden/.

2. Buchan, *The Thirty-Nine Steps*, gutenberg.org/ ebooks/558.

3. Drori, *Around the World in 80 Trees*, 212.

4. Wikipedia, s.v. "Powys Thomas," en.wikipedia. org/wiki/Powys_Thomas.

5. Bill Stephen, "Ornamental Trees of Stanley Park," in *Wilderness on the Doorstep*, ed. Robinson.

6. Two of Sir Harry Lauder's books are available at gutenberg.org.

CHAPTER 28

1. *Sister and Seven Brothers*, news reel, 1924, British Pathé, britishpathe.com/video/sister-and-seven-brothers/query/%22Sister+And+S even+Brothers%22.

CHAPTER 29

1. "Vancouver Board of Parks and Recreation," Your Government, City of Vancouver, vancouver.ca/your-government/vancouver-board-of-parks-and-recreation.aspx.

2. "Vancouver Board of Parks and Recreation Offices," Canada's Historic Places, historicplaces.ca/en/rep-reg/place-lieu. aspx?id=8824.

3. Ibid.

CHAPTER 30

1. Wikipedia, s.v. "Rhododendron," en.wikipedia.org/wiki/Rhododendron.

2. Don Benson and Alleyne Cook, "Trees and Shrubs of Stanley Park: English Bay to Lost Lagoon," in *The Natural History of Stanley Park*, ed. Vancouver Natural History Society (Vancouver, BC: Discovery Press, 1988).

3. See "Ted and Mary Greig Rhododendron Garden" at vancouver.ca/parks-recreation-culture/gardens-in-stanley-park.aspx. You can download three PDFs: *50 Rhododendrons of Interest*, *50 Trees and Shrubs of Interest*, and a calendar of when different species bloom. These PDFs have some spelling errors.

4. *Vancouver Sun*, "Barbara Cook Magnolia," interview with Barbara and Alleyne Cook about Magnolia 'Barbara Cook,' YouTube video, youtube.com/watch?v=B7wpvhRrSUg.

CHAPTER 31

1. Steele, *First 100 Years*, 213.

2. Posts tagged with "A.G. Ferguson," *Changing Vancouver* (blog), changingvancouver.word-press.com/tag/a-g-ferguson/.

3. Matthews, *Early Vancouver*, 1:218. Major Matthews interviewed W.H. Gallagher on December 30, 1931.

4. For photos of the fire truck after it was .repaired in 2011, see Vancouver Board of Parks and Recreation, "2011-04-27 fire truck returns to Stanley Park," Facebook photo album, April 2011, facebook.com/pg/parkboard/photos/?tab=album&album_id=10150559792155230.

CHAPTER 32

1. Sue Bigelow, "The Robert Burns Memorial in Stanley Park," *AuthentiCity* (City of Vancouver Archives blog), vancouverarchives.ca/2014/01/24/the-robert-burns-memorial-in-stanley-park/.

2. "Our Mission and Vision," About Us, Stanley Park Ecology Society, stanley-parkecology.ca/about-us/our-history/our-mission-and-vision/.

3. "Beaver Lake Needs Your Input at Open Houses!," Conservation, Stanley Park Ecology Society, stanleyparkecology.ca/2013/11/15/beaver-lake-needs-input-open-houses-week/.

4. Invasive Species Council of BC, *Invasive Species Strategy for British Columbia: 2017-2022* (Williams Lake, BC: Invasive Species Council of BC, 2017), bcinvasives.ca/documents/Invasive_Species_Strategy_2017_2022_171019_WEB.pdf.

5. "Volunteer," Get Involved, Stanley Park Ecology Society, stanleyparkecology.ca/get-involved/volunteer/.

CHAPTER 33

1. Matthews, *Early Vancouver*, 4:202.

2. Steele, *First 100 Years*, 212.

3. Matthews, *Early Vancouver*, 4:203. The parentheses are Major Matthews's.

4. Ibid., 6:94.

EPILOGUE

1. Suzanne Simard, "How Trees Talk to Each Other," filmed June 2016, TED video, 18:20, ted.com/talks/suzanne_simard_how_trees_talk_to_each_other.

2. Terri Clark, "Some Trees of Greater Vancouver," *Discover Vancouver*, archive.li/BS5hi.

3. Steve Whysall, "Alleyne Cook: Up Close and Personal," October 31, 2013, *Vancouver Sun*, vancouversun.com/news/staff-blogs/alleyne-cook-up-close-and-personal.

4. See also a companion to the list in the book, at UBC Botanical Garden, *Trees and Shrubs of Stanley Park: English Bay to Lost Lagoon*, (Vancouver, BC: UBC Botanical Garden, 2010), forums.botanicalgarden.ubc.ca/attachments/naturalhistorytreesstanleyparkbylocation-pdf.82431.

5. "Stanley Park National Historic Site of Canada," Canada's Historic Places, his-toricplaces.ca/en/rep-reg/place-lieu.aspx?id=12546&pid=0.

6. Parks Canada and National Historic Sites of Canada, *Stanley Park National Historic Site of Canada: Commemorative Integrity Statement* (Ottawa, ON: Parks Canada and National Historic Sites of Canada, 2002), stanleyparkecology.ca/wp-content/uploads/downloads/2012/02/ParksCanada_Commemorative-Integrity-Statement-2002.pdf.

7. Treepedia, Vancouver, senseable.mit.edu/treepedia/cities/Vancouver.

8. When my surname was Woolliams, I wrote *Cattle Ranch: The Story of the Douglas Lake Cattle Company* (Vancouver, BC: Douglas & McIntyre, 1979). Having left Wales, a country steeped in centuries of history, I was captured by the tangible history of my new home. I spent seven years researching Douglas Lake Cattle Company's history and two more years writing it. I truly resonate with Major Matthews's fascination with a new homeland.

9. See searcharchives.vancouver.ca.

Sources and Recommended Reading

Barman, Jean. *Stanley Park's Secret: The Forgotten Families of Whoi Whoi, Kanaka Ranch and Brockton Point.* Madeira Park, BC: Harbour, 2005.

Buchan, John. *The Thirty-Nine Steps.* Edinburgh: William Blackwood and Sons, 1915; Project Gutenberg, 2008. gutenberg.org/ebooks/558.

Chamovitz, Daniel. *What a Plant Knows: A Field Guide to the Senses.* New York: Scientific American Books, 2013.

Davies, John. *Douglas of the Forests: The North American Journals of David Douglas.* Seattle: University of Washington Press, 1980.

Davis, Chuck, ed. *The Greater Vancouver Book: An Urban Encyclopedia.* Surrey, BC: Linkman Press, 1997.

Douglas, David. *Journal Kept by David Douglas, 1823-1827.* London: William, Wesley & Son, 1914; Biodiversity Heritage Library, 2006. biodiversitylibrary.org/item/59487#page/4/mode/1up.

Drori, Jonathan. *Around the World in 80 Trees.* London, UK: Laurence King, 2018.

Fara, Patricia. *Sex, Botany and Empire: The Story of Carl Linnaeus and Joseph Banks.* London: Icon Books, 2003.

Government of British Columbia. Glossary of Forestry Terms. www.for.gov.bc.ca/hfd/library/documents/glossary/1990s/index.htm.

Johnson, E. Pauline. *Legends of Vancouver.* New York: Mythik Press, 1913; Project Gutenberg, 2004. gutenberg.org/ebooks/3478.

Justice, Douglas. *Ornamental Cherries in Vancouver.* Vancouver, BC: UBC Botanical Garden and the Vancouver Cherry Blossom Festival, 2014.

Ketchum, Richard M. *The Secret Life of the Forest*, New York: McGraw-Hill, 1970; e-book New Word City, 1st edition, 2017.

Matthews, Major James Skitt. *Early Vancouver*, 7 vols. 1932 to 1956. Transcription of the first edition, including handwritten marginalia and corrections made by the author. Vancouver, BC: City of Vancouver, 2011. former.vancouver.ca/ctyclerk/archives/digitized/EarlyVan/index.htm and vancouver.ca/your-government/major-matthews-early-vancouver.aspx.

———. *Vancouver Historic Journal*. Vancouver, BC: Vancouver City Archives, 1958.

McCarthy, James. *Monkey Puzzle Man: Archibald Menzies, Plant Hunter*. Dunbeath, UK: Whittles, 2008.

Menzies, Archibald. *Menzies' Journal of Vancouver's Voyage: April to October, 1792*. Edited by C.F. Newcombe, MD. Victoria, BC: Legislative Assembly of British Columbia, 1923. open.library.ubc.ca/collections/bcbooks/items/1.0226118 and archive.org/details/menziesjournalof1792menz/.

Muir, John. *The Yosemite*. New York, 1912; Project Gutenberg, 2003. gutenberg.org/ebooks/7091.

National Parks and National Historic Sites of Canada. *Stanley Park: National Historic Site of Canada: Commemorative Integrity Statement*. Vancouver, BC: Parks Canada, Vancouver Board of Parks and Recreation, 2002. stanleyparkecology.ca/wp-content/uploads/downloads/2012/02/ParksCanada_Commemorative-Integrity-Statement-2002.pdf.

Parish, Roberta, and Sandra Thomson. *Tree Book: Learning to Recognize Trees of British Columbia*. Victoria, BC: British Columbia Ministry of Forests, Land and Natural Resource Operations; Ottawa, ON: Canadian Forest Service; 1995. www.for.gov.bc.ca/hfd/library/documents/treebook/.

Parkinson, Alison, ed. *Wilderness on the Doorstep: Discovering Nature in Stanley Park*. Madeira Park, BC: Harbour, 2006.

Pojar, Jim, and Andy MacKinnon. *Plants of Coastal British Columbia including Washington Oregon and Alaska*. Vancouver, BC: Lone Pine, 1994.

Sleigh, Daphne. *The Man Who Saved Vancouver: Major James Skitt Matthews*. Surrey, BC: Heritage House, 2008.

Steele, Mike R. *The First 100 Years: The Vancouver Board of Parks and Recreation; An Illustrated Celebration*. Vancouver, BC: Vancouver Board of Parks and Recreation, 1988.

Straley, Gerald B. *Trees of Vancouver: A Guide to the Common and Unusual Trees of the City*. Vancouver, BC: UBC Press, 1992.

Suzuki, David, Wayne Grady, and Robert Bateman. *Tree: A Life Story*. Vancouver, BC: Greystone Books and David Suzuki Foundation, 2007.

Tracey, David. *Vancouver Tree Book: A Living City Field Guide*. Vancouver, BC: Pure Wave Media, 2016. davidtracey.ca/product/vancouver-tree-book-ebook/.

Vancouver, Captain George. *A Voyage of Discovery to the North Pacific Ocean, and Round the World*. 3 vols. London: G.G. and J. Robinson, Paternoster Row, and J. Edwards, Pall Mall, 1798; Internet Archive, 2011. archive.org/details/voyageofdiscover01vanc/page/n7.

Vancouver Natural History Society. *The Natural History of Stanley Park*, Vancouver, BC: Discovery Press, 1988.

Vancouver Parks and Recreation. *Stanley Park Forest Management Plan*. Vancouver, BC: Vancouver Parks and Recreation, 2009. vancouver.ca/files/cov/Stanley-Park-Forest-Management-Plan.pdf.

Wohlleben, Peter. *The Hidden Life of Trees: What They Feel, How They Communicate; Discoveries from a Secret World*. Vancouver, BC: Greystone Books, 2018.

WEBSITES AND APPS

City of Vancouver—Gardens in Stanley Park. Download three brochures on Ted and Mary Greig Rhododendron Garden trees from vancouver.ca/parks-recreation-culture/gardens-in-stanley-park.aspx.

City of Vancouver Archives, searcharchives.vancouver.ca.

The History of Metropolitan Vancouver, vancouverhistory.ca. The website was founded by the journalist and broadcaster Chuck Davis.

History of Stanley Park, vancouver.ca/parks-recreation-culture/stanley-park-history.aspx.

Public Art Registry, covapp.vancouver.ca/PublicArtRegistry/HomePage.aspx.

"Some Trees of Greater Vancouver" by Terri Clark, *Discover Vancouver*. archive.li/BS5hi.

Stanley Park Ecology Society's ecology reports, 1994 to today. stanleyparkecology.ca/news-and-resources/publications/stanley-park-ecology-reports/.

Treepedia (Vancouver), senseable.mit.edu/treepedia/cities/Vancouver.

Vancouver Big Tree Hiking Guide, vancouversbigtrees.com. This website is run by Ira Sutherland.

Vancouver Heritage Register, vancouver.ca/files/cov/V001-vancouver-heritage-register-june-2014.pdf.

Vancouver Street Trees, data.vancouver.ca/data-catalogue/streetTrees.htm.

Vancouver Trees app. University of British Columbia, 2015.

Way of the Dreamer, mossdreams.com. Episodes of Robert Moss's radio program can be found at healthylife.net/RadioShow/archiveWD.htm.

Index